THE LIGHTS ARE WAR

First presented by The City Missouri in 1969. First performance in Britain at the Pitlochry Festival Theatre on 8th June 1979 with the following cast:

Emma Borden	Moira Lamb
Maggie	Charmaine Parsons
Nance O'Neil	Sarah Neville
Tom Fuller	Michael Mackenzie
Annie Beale	Mavis Taylor-Blake
Henry Webb	David Sterne
Lizzie Borden	Beverley Walding
The Visitor	Anne White

Directed by Brian Shelton
Designed by Colin Winslow

The action takes place in the living-room of "Maplecroft"—a large house in Fall River, Massachusetts, USA.

ACT I   An autumn evening
ACT II About half an hour later

Time: 1905

ACT I

The living-room at "Maplecroft", in Fall River, Massachusetts. An evening in autumn, 1905

The house is a large one; all the furniture and trappings are homely and well cared for. A slight dais leads to the french windows, which open on to a garden. At present the curtains are drawn across, save for a strip where they meet. See plan on p. 56

As the CURTAIN *rises Emma Borden is discovered sitting embroidering a handkerchief. She is a slightly plump woman of fifty-six. Her dress and manner are sombre. A knock is heard on the front door, followed by a babble of voices and laughter*

Emma Maggie!

A moment elapses, during which another burst of laughter is heard. Emma stops sewing and looks a little impatient

Maggie!

A further knocking is heard, and Emma is about to get up

Maggie enters. She is an untidy, slovenly—but rather pretty—maid, aged twenty-two

Open the door!

Maggie (*sighing*) Yes, Miss Emma. (*She goes and opens the front door*)

Four of the "artistes" from the local theatre enter, led by Nance O'Neil, a flamboyant actress aged thirty-one, with red hair and a husky voice. Tom Fuller is a good-looking actor, with dark hair, of about the same age. Annie Beale is attractive, rather than pretty, with blonde hair and large blue eyes. She is twenty-two. Henry Webb is a slightly portly man, of average height, and takes his acting seriously. He is in his late thirties. Nance makes an entrance by sailing across to Emma, her hand outstretched

Nance You're dear Lizzie's sister. I'd have recognized you anywhere. Glad to know you, Emma.

Emma (*unenthusiastically*) You must be Miss O'Neil.

Nance Call me Nance.

Emma Where is my sister?

Nance She stopped along the sidewalk, but said for us to come on ahead, and meet you, because she'd be along directly. Isn't that so, Tom?

Tom She picked up a stray cat. It was sick. Just outside the theatre.

Nance It must a' seen your performance. (*She laughs loudly at this*) But I'm forgetting my manners. This is Miss Emma Borden, everyone. (*To*

Emma) And this is Tom Fuller. (*In an exaggerated aside*) If he acted half as well on the stage as he acts off it, we'd never be able to afford him.

Tom Pleased to meet you, Miss Emma. Have you been to see the play down at the theatre?

Emma I'm afraid I don't enjoy such entertainments.

Nance Hell! Who's talking about entertainment? We're talking about watching Tom, here, act. (*She laughs again*)

Emma is tongue-tied, and looks to the door, as if hoping Lizzie will soon relieve her of playing hostess

Emma Well—I mean—I . . .

Nance (*nudging Emma*) Don't mind me. It's just artistic temperament, if you know what I mean? You must a' read about it, somewhere. And this, here, is Annie Beale. Come and say hello to the nice lady, Annie. (*In a loud whisper*) She's a mite shy.

Annie (*defiantly*) How do you do, Miss Borden?

Nance Now, that wasn't very *ingénue*, was it? (*To Emma*) And last, and by all means least, meet Henry Webb. Henry's mission in life is searching out truth. Don't ask me what he intends doing with it when he finds it. Should it fail to drown him first, that is.

Henry smiles, and cynically applauds

Henry Game and first set to Miss Nance O'Neil, who's upstaged the lot of us from the moment we first set foot in the house. (*To Emma*) I'm sure pleased to meet you, ma'am. Take no notice of Nance. She's a little cantankerous this week because she wasn't permitted to play the lead at the theatre.

Emma (*politely*) What is the title of the piece?

Tom *The Hound of the Baskervilles.*

Nance smiles

Emma (*to Henry*) An interesting novel. Do you play Mr Sherlock Holmes?

Henry No.

Nance He's too fat, honey.

Tom Besides, it needs an actor of my calibre.

Henry I play Doctor Watson.

Emma They are both very clever characters. Lizzie and I have read most of the stories.

Nance Imagine!

Emma Do you suppose the English police are really like that?

Henry Of course not. This is fiction.

Nance (*with a mock sigh*) You are going to be sorry you ever asked that question, Emma. Can't you see him about to leap on to his hobby-horse, shouting "The truth, the truth, my kingdom for the truth"?

Annie (*slightly more boldly*) Just because he looks for the truth in order to apply it to his performances and give them a little freshness, instead of relying on a sackful of old hand-me-down clichés, is no reason for— for . . . (*She flounders*)

Nance Where's the prompt? (*With a sugary smile*) It's my experience that life, itself, is a sackful of old hand-me-down clichés. And dat, honey chile, is de truth!

Henry (*picking up where he left off*) True policemen aren't as infallible as Messrs Holmes and Watson. Nor do they have such highly improbable crimes to solve. In real life there's less—premeditation. Murder happens in the heat of the moment. An innocent morning—everyone moving about in daylight—no house on the moors—nor stormy night—but with ordinary people planning for a tomorrow they will never see. That's murder. That's when death strikes . . .!

Henry makes a slicing movement with the side of one hand, hitting the palm of the other. The noise causes Emma to shudder, and he becomes aware that her face presents a stony mask—that she has withdrawn from the conversation. There is a short silence. Nance comes to the rescue

Nance Naturally, we don't always play pieces of this kind.

Tom Remember *The Stubbornness of Geraldine*?

Nance Remember it? It will haunt me for the rest of my days! (*To Emma*) It was the sentimental comedy to end all sentimental comedies. I preferred the burlesque they did in New York. *The Stickiness of Gelatine.* It was more . . .

Emma does not seem to be listening to this conversation, but is deep in thought. She places a hand to her forehead, and stands up

Emma Do forgive me—I've a headache—and my cologne . . .

Emma hurriedly leaves the room

Nance You're a fool, Henry! A fat fool!

Henry I wasn't directly referring to . . . (*He shrugs his shoulders*) Besides, how should I know she'd be so sensitive after all this time?

Tom It's over ten years, Nance.

Nance Thirteen, to be precise. But you don't forget an experience like that. It's not like a—a fall down the stairs, you know. (*Pause*) Both parents!

Tom But Emma wasn't even accused of the murders. Lizzie was the one they tried.

Nance Nevertheless, they were Emma's parents, too. (*Reflectively*) For both of them to die like that!

Annie It's like treading on ice, if we're to avoid saying anything that might —remind them of it. We shouldn't a' come.

Henry Annie's right. Why did you bring us here, Nance?

Nance Because I promised. I was playing a summer resort last year—and I met Lizzie, who was kind enough to invite me to her home—so I told her I'd be glad of a visit should I ever play Fall River. Well, here I am. Besides, I'm not going to pretend to be blasé. I find it exciting knowing Lizzie Borden. Enigmas fascinate me.

Annie (*child-like in her excitement*) Do you think Lizzie did it, Nance?

Pause

Nance You've met her. What do you think?

Pause

Annie She certainly doesn't seem the type to kill her folks with an axe, and that's the truth!

Henry The truth is, she was acquitted. (*Slight pause*) But, of course, that doesn't mean to say she didn't do it.

Annie (*excitedly*) You think she did?

Pause

Henry I don't know. The case has—aspects . . .

Tom Does it really matter whether she did it or not?

Nance Depends who you are, doesn't it? For myself, she's more interesting as an unknown quantity. But Henry, here, wants no truck with unknown quantities. All he wants is truth. Plain, unvarnished, dull ol' truth. (*She casts a momentary wicked glance at Annie*) It makes for a very unromantic lover. After all, no romance is complete without a little frivolous, thoroughly fictitious flattery!

Annie is embarrassed by this reference. Tom notices, and turns sharply to Nance

Tom And what is that supposed to mean?

Nance Ah! Sir Galahad to the rescue.

Tom Well?

Nance Guinevere knows what I'm talking about. Don't you, dear?

Annie turns away—Nance returns to Tom

Or did you wish to discuss unromantic lovers in more detail?

This is a pointed remark, and Tom prefers to ignore its implication

Tom We were talking about Lizzie Borden.

Nance (*tauntingly, in a loud whisper*) Why don't we talk about us? Eh, Tom? And how I was thrown aside like a worn-out theatrical cliché? (*She laughs, and goes across to the table where she helps herself to some of the food that has been set out for them*) But, if you insist on talking about Lizzie, then I must confess I don't know whether she did it or not. (*Slight pause—then with a quizzical expression*) Maybe it'd be interesting to know—(*she pauses, smiles and bows to Henry*)—the truth! (*Pause*) Maybe no-one'll ever know. (*Pause*) I think I'd rather that no-one ever knew. I guess I'll go on having respect for Mother Nature for just so long as she goes on holding out on me with a few things. (*She busies herself with some punch*) Anyhow, you've all read up on the trial. Surely one of you must have come up with some kind of opinion as to whether or not she . . .

The front door slams and Nance becomes silent

Lizzie Borden enters. She looks something like her sister, but is younger— namely, forty-five. She is dressed in an attractive blue dress over which she wears a short cape. When she wishes to scrutinize anything she puts on a

*pair of pince-nez, which she wears around her neck on a thin black cord.
Her voice and manner are undramatic as she busies herself with removing
hat, cape and gloves, and putting each article away neatly, talking all the
while*

Lizzie Good evening, folks. My! What a sudden silence, Nance. A voice
stopping in mid-flight. It's not like you at all, is it? Do I detect a hint
of—forbidden conversation—in the air? It's not really forbidden, you
know. Talk your head off, if you want. After all, it's not as if the episode
will ever be allowed to completely rest. Conversations will often stop as
I enter a room. There'll always be some child at the end of some street,
ready to chant about how Lizzie Borden took her axe and gave her
mother forty whacks! (*She moves to the buffet supper on the table*) Lord
above! I thought actors had appetites like hogs. Don't none of you
want to eat? (*She looks about her*) What happened to Emma?

*The rest of the group move to the table, and Lizzie helps them to cups of
punch*

Nance Henry was a little tactless.
Lizzie (*smiling*) Forbidden conversation?
Nance (*nodding*) Forbidden conversation.

They laugh

Lizzie Poor Henry! You weren't to know. She's sensitive. Particularly
with regard to "theatricals". You're all treading the primrose path, and
she don't aim to be swept alongside of you. (*She helps herself to food*)
What, exactly, did you say?
Nance He was theorizing about—crime—and, in particular to—in
particular to . . .
Lizzie Murder?
Nance (*apologetically*) Yes.
Lizzie Then say it! For heaven's sake, Nance. It's just a word. Say it!
Murder!

Annie watches Lizzie, fascinated, during the above. This amuses Lizzie

Do I shock you, young lady?
Annie (*bashfully*) Well—perhaps a little . . .
Lizzie You're Annie, aren't you?
Annie That's right.
Lizzie Listen, Annie. I learned two things from my father. Thrift—of
which I'm not really proud—and honesty, of which I am. Maybe
"honesty" isn't the right word, but "bluntness". Yes. Bluntness. He
taught me that. When he said something he said it in no uncertain terms.
And I admired him for it.

Emma enters

Emma I thought I heard you come in.
Nance How's the headache?

Emma Headache? (*Remembering*) Oh, much better, thank you. (*To Lizzie*) What did you do with the sick cat?

Slight pause

Lizzie It seemed as if its paw was trodden on, so I cleaned it as best I could, and tied my handkerchief over it. Then I thought to bring it home with me until the paw was a little better, so I picked up the poor creature. Just at that moment one of the women who's new to the town came over—she'd been watching all the time—and said, "Excuse me, but ain't you Lizzie Borden?" I told her that was so, and she snatched the cat from my arms—as if from the jaws of hell—and made off with it!

Emma (*distressed*) We should a' moved away from the town, Liz . . .

Lizzie Not that the action of the woman bothered me. What I did find a little—curious—was the feeling there was somebody else there— watching me . . .

Tom Did you see anyone?

Lizzie (*shrugging*) I don't know. Maybe a shadow . . . Then I had the strange feeling of being followed home . . .

Tom But, again, you saw no-one?

Lizzie I looked back once or twice—but it was dark . . .

Emma We should a' moved away, like I said. Changed our names, and moved away. (*She sits*)

Lizzie If that's what you want, Emma, you go ahead. But not me. I don't figure living a lie for the rest of my days.

Nance Good for you, Lizzie, gal! (*To Emma*) Lizzie's right, honey.

Annie What did she think you were doing with the animal?

Lizzie (*laughing*) I think they look on me as a kind of a witch.

Emma That's no laughing matter.

Tom Of course it is. Witches! In this year of nineteen hundred and five!

Emma (*withdrawing into herself*) You don't understand how we think or feel in Fall River. I guess it comes from us being—"provincials" . . . (*Tight-lipped, she attacks her embroidery with renewed vigour*)

Lizzie ignores this tiny outburst, as though used to such storms

Lizzie (*smiling*) One small boy always crosses to the other side of the street if he passes this house. Like a ritual. Automatically, he crosses over to the other side. (*She ponders on this for a moment*) It'd sure be worth something to know what kind of a tale his folks have told him.

Tom (*to Emma*) I wasn't laughing at you. I just didn't figure people still believed in magic, and all that stuff. I mean—well—we do some mighty astonishing things in the theatre—like me playing Mephistopheles, and disappearing in a cloud of smoke . . . But people know it's a trick. Some even write to ask how I do it.

Emma concentrates on her needlework, determinedly

Annie (*to Lizzie, surprised*) Is life here difficult for you still?

Lizzie Most of the folks pay me no heed.

Emma (*sharply, not looking up from her work*) Why should they? Lizzie didn't do it. She was acquitted.

Lizzie A few still think I was guilty.
Henry When they acquitted you, did they not try finding someone else . . .
Nance Henry! You know we shouldn't talk . . .

Lizzie quietens her with a wave of her hand

Lizzie You know, Henry, you're jumping to exactly the same conclusion as most others. Namely, that I was the only suspect, and that no-one else was questioned. I just happened to be suspect number one. The most likeliest person.
Emma (*impulsively*) I could just as easily a' done it, you know.
Lizzie That is simply not true, Emma. You were staying with friends in Fairhaven at the time.
Henry How far away is Fairhaven?
Lizzie (*shrugging her shoulders*) A little over fifteen miles, I guess. Not from here, you understand, but from the house where it happened. We moved here afterwards. It's a better part of town.
Emma (*persistently*) There were regular trains from Fairhaven. I could easily a' made it. Nobody checked on me.
Lizzie It just wasn't necessary, Emma. We both know you didn't do it, don't we?
Annie (*slowly*) You—both—know—she didn't do it?

Lizzie frowns, sees the implication of the remark, and laughs

Lizzie Thank heaven you weren't on that jury!
Annie (*shamefacedly*) I'm sorry. I misunderstood . . .
Emma (*peckingly*) My sister has some fool notion she knows who did it.
Nance (*excitedly*) Is that so, Lizzie?
Emma And goes around telling folk—at least, those who still talk to us.
Lizzie How you do exaggerate, Emma. I mentioned it, in confidence, to Alice . . .
Emma Supposing the murderer's still in town, and gets to hear . . .
Lizzie The murderer's not in town, but far away, as I've told you before. (*To Nance*) Emma's afraid he'll come after me if he thinks I really know his identity.
Henry If you think you really do know his identity, why don't you go to the police?
Lizzie To what purpose?
Annie It's dangerous, leaving a murderer loose like that.

Lizzie thoughtfully shakes her head

Lizzie I think not. After all, it was thirteen years ago, and it hasn't happened again, has it?
Emma Huh! It don't mean to say it can't!
Henry Aren't you interested in presenting the public with . . . (*He pauses, and looks at Nance*)
Nance The truth, Henry? Go on, say it.
Henry (*without rancour*) Why is it, Nance, that the word "truth" always sounds so ugly when uttered by you?

Nance I guess because I was always the child who bawled when they stripped the tinsel from the tree. I knew what lay beneath the glitter, Henry. I just didn't need to see it.

Henry (*returning to the point of digression*) But aren't you interested in clearing your name, Miss Lizzie?

Lizzie Who's to say they could prove my suspicions?

Emma Besides, we don't want that vicious publicity all over again. It was terrible. *The Fall River Globe* was real nasty to poor Lizzie.

Lizzie Anyway, there's a flaw to my theory.

Henry What's that?

Lizzie Motive.

Annie So you don't really know who did it?

Lizzie I didn't say that, Annie. I said I don't know why they did it. But they did it, all right.

Annie "They"?

Lizzie He, or she. I've no intention of handing you a name.

Emma She won't even tell me.

Lizzie If I told you, Emma, you'd be down at the station, hurling accusations, before I'd had time to flee the country! (*She laughs*)

Annie Don't you hate . . .?

Lizzie Let's say, "him".

Annie Don't you hate him—for what he did to your father and mother?

Lizzie (*matter-of-factly*) She was my stepmother.

Annie Don't you—

Lizzie It was a long time ago. Neither was very close to me—particularly her. (*Pause, reflectively*) To tell the truth, Annie, I've never really posed the question. Whether or not I hate the killer, that is.(*Pause*) No. There's no hate. (*Pause*) Pity, perhaps, that someone should be so—evil.

Henry Do you suspect someone inside the house?

Lizzie (*drily*) He was certainly inside at the time of the crimes.

Emma (*shocked*) Lizzie! How can you joke about it?

Lizzie Because I'm not sensitive, dear. Like you're always telling me.

Emma becomes even more tight-lipped as she withers at the remark. Lizzie relents a little

Sorry, Emma. I know it's no joking matter.

Emma (*to Nance, accusingly*) You shouldn't talk about it.

Nance I'd be far happier talking about me, honey, but who's in the teeniest bit interested in hearing the life story of the most brilliant actress this side of eternity?

Lizzie (*to Emma, gently*) Doesn't it occur to you I might want to talk about it sometimes?

Emma (*reluctantly*) Well, of course, if you want to . . .

Emma shrugs her shoulders and concentrates on her work. Lizzie looks at her sister's bowed head, smiles wryly, and turns to Nance

Lizzle (*reflectively*) Our stepmother—Abby, as Emma always preferred to call her—never meant any more to us, I guess, than that she married our father when our real mother died. Wouldn't you say that, Emma? (*Pause*) Cat got your tongue?

Emma (*shortly*) You were more her friend than I was.

Lizzie What she really means is, that I was able to be civil to her! (*Pause*) Not that I remember my real mother. She died when I was two years old.

Annie (*excitedly*) Was your stepmother wicked, like in all the stories?

Lizzie No! I was no Cinderella.

Annie (*disappointedly*) Oh, I thought she'd be thin, and real mean-looking.

Nance Heavens, Annie! She was a wholesome, homely-looking woman. Two hundred pounds she weighed. And just over five feet high. Like a great india-rubber ball.

Lizzie How come you know so much about her, Nance?

Nance I read, don't I?

Tom You hear that, Henry? The lady reads.

Henry Surely you don't mean Nance?

Tom The very same.

Henry But does she comprehend what she reads? Answer me that, Tom.

Tom I'm afraid you got me, there, fella.

Nance Why don't you two boys go for a nice long walk? To Nebraska, for instance. (*To Lizzie*) Go on, honey. You were telling us about your stepmother.

Pause

Lizzie She meant well. (*A pause. She laughs*) Sometimes I reckon that's the most awful thing one person can say about another. (*She laughs again*) Nevertheless, in this instance it happened to be true.

Emma Meant well for who?

Lizzie Everyone.

Emma (*contemptuously*) Huh! For her own side of the family.

Lizzie That's just not fair, Emma. Nor, indeed, is it completely true. And well you know it.

Emma You were too young to understand, at the time. You didn't see how—how conniving she was. How she—inveigled Father into marrying her.

Lizzie You saw it only because you wanted to.

Annie (*excitedly*) Please tell us about it! The—the—well, you know—everything!

Emma (*contemptuously*) Sensation-seekers! But I guess one shouldn't expect more from—from theatricals!

Lizzie (*rebukingly*) Emma!

Emma bows her head to her work

Nance We don't mind, Lizzie. Really. Emma's quite entitled to her opinion. In some towns we're treated like pariahs.

Annie I'm sorry. It was my fault.

Lizzie (*kindly but firmly*) You are my guests, and we will talk about the things you are interested in talking about. If my sister Emma disapproves, she doesn't have to stay.

Annie (*distressed*) Oh, I don't want to cause you to quarrel . . .

Lizzie We don't exactly quarrel. Just spit for a moment or two. (*She laughs*) It's what a couple of elderly ladies do to break the monotony every now and then. We don't have many visitors. (*She helps herself to another glass of punch. Reflectively*) Sometimes it seems to have happened fifty years ago. Others it appears only a matter of weeks. Yet it was thirteen years. August fourth, eighteen ninety-two. At ninety-two, Second Street, Fall River, Massachusetts. Just after eleven a.m. A hot, sunny morning—like any other hot, sunny morning—at least, for other folk it was—not for the Borden family. Emma was away in Fairhaven . . .

During the above the Lights dim on all save Lizzie

Emma (*stubbornly, from the darkness*) I could a' got there! Nobody checked.

Lizzie (*firmly*) Emma was in Fairhaven, as I told you. Maggie—the maid— was in her room. Taking a mid-morning rest. I had been outside, in the barn, and went back into the house . . .

The Lights dim on Lizzie, and a spot comes up on Annie

Annie Oh, I can just imagine it—I shudder to think of it—a large house, full of shadows—and smelling of evil—and death—and this poor woman entering from the barn . . . (*Her voice trails off. Trance-like to begin with, she goes through the motions of entering a room, finding a man brutally murdered on a couch, throwing herself on to her knees beside him. It is very melodramatic*) Father! Who did this . . . ?

Terrified, Annie moves away from the body, gives a slight scream, and begins running, shaking her head as if to throw out the scene she has just witnessed. Lizzie's laugh breaks the scene

Lizzie It wasn't a bit like that, Annie.

Annie But that's how it was when we did *The Crime at Corley Castle*.

Nance Yes. I felt I'd seen that performance before. Does Lizzie strike you as the kind who'd react in that manner?

Annie Well, I hadn't thought . . .

Nance You never do, honey. The style was too theatrical. Look, Annie. You play the maid—if she's needed—and leave Lizzie to me.

Playfully, Nance pushes Annie out of the lighted area, and a moment later she herself enters. But now it is a different Nance. An actress successfully playing a role. She has adopted Lizzie's walk, mannerisms, and—to an extent—her voice. She goes through the motions of walking through a yard, picking a flower, looking up at the sky, brushing at her skirt, and entering a house. Once inside, she enters a room, unsuspectingly, and discovers the murder. Her reaction is shocked, and quiet. Haltingly, she moves closer to the body—then walks sharply to the "door" and calls up the "stairs"

Maggie, come down!

Annie (*from the darkness, with an Irish accent*) What is the matter?
Nance Come down quick. (*Unbelievingly*) Father's dead. (*She moves back and looks into the room. Her voice is hoarse*) Somebody came in and killed him.

Annie rushes into the circle of light, and is about to enter the murder room, but Nance bars her way

I have got to have a doctor. Hurry, Maggie!
Annie But But Miss Lizzie, I . . .
Nance (*firmly*) I have got to have a doctor. Go!

Annie rushes off from the lighted area. Nance paces about in the circle of light, her features thoughtful, and every now and then glances toward the murder room. Once, she puts her hands to her eyes, as if to brush away a tear—but the movement is indefinite, and might be merely a nervous gesture. Annie appears, breathless

Annie Doctor Bowen's not at home, Miss Lizzie, but Mrs Bowen says he'll not be long.

Nance looks about her for an alternative to the doctor

Nance Which of my friends . . . ? (*Nervously she drums her fingers. Sharply*) Go get Miss Russell. Quickly. I don't want to be in this house alone.

Annie rushes off from the lighted area. Nance paces a little, then goes through the motions of drawing back a curtain and looking through a window. She catches sight of someone

Oh, Mrs Churchill, do come over. Quickly!

After a moment Annie appears—this time as Mrs Churchill

Thank heavens you've come, Mrs Churchill. Someone has killed Father. He's in there.

Nance points in the direction of the room. Annie looks at the "body" and is appalled. There is a slight pause before she speaks

Annie Where were you when it happened?
Nance I went to the barn to get a piece of iron. Father must have an enemy for we have all been sick, and we think the bread has been poisoned. (*She paces, then turns, impulsively*) A doctor! I must have a doctor!
Annie Are you sure you'll be all right?
Nance Yes. Go get one.

Annie goes off from the lighted area again and Nance sits on the edge of the dais, her hands over her face

Lizzie (*from the darkness*) Two days before that, my father, stepmother and myself had all been sick during the night.
Emma Abby reckoned it was poison, and wanted to see Dr Bowen.
Tom Did she see him?

Lizzie She went across secretly.

Tom Why secretly?

Henry (*his voice hard*) It costs money, Abby. Well, my money shan't pay for it!

Tom What did the doctor say?

Lizzie He just laughed.

The Lights dim on Nance, and go up on Annie—still playing Mrs Churchill, as she walks rapidly across the street. She sees someone

Annie Oh, Mr Cunningham . . .?

Tom moves into the light, and tips an imaginary hat

Tom What can I do for you, Mrs Churchill?

Annie Will you please go fetch a doctor? It's very urgent. Send him to the Borden house.

Tom Sure thing.

Annie moves away, leaving Tom alone in the light. He frowns as he watches her go, then goes through the actions of dialling a number on a telephone

Is that the *Daily Globe*? . . . John Cunningham speaking. Thought you'd like to know there's trouble in the Borden household. They've sent me for a doctor . . . Yeah, well you won't forget where you got the information, will you? (*He hangs up, and dials another number*) Marshall Hilliard? . . . John Cunningham here . . . Listen! There's some kind of trouble down at the Borden place. I'm on my way to find a doctor . . . That's O.K. Just thought you ought to know. (*He hangs up and moves off, out of his light-spot*)

Lizzie (*wrily*) Ultimately, of course, he went for a doctor!

Annie moves into the light and just stands there, puzzled

Nance (*after a pause*) Well? What are you waiting for?

The main Lights come up

Annie I've forgotten who I am.

Nance There are times I wonder how I retain my sanity. You are Alice Russell. My friend, Alice Russell. Remember now?

Annie But I'm Maggie, who went for her. (*She suddenly remembers herself, and repeats her line with an Irish accent*) I'm Maggie, who'd be after going for her. (*Pause*) And Mrs Churchill.

Nance (*imitating Annie's Irish accent*) You wouldn't be toying with the notion of playing all three parts at the same time, now, would ye?

Annie What about the others when they come back? Who'll play them?

Nance (*in her own voice*) We'll try to be clever enough not to bring them all on together. Meanwhile, you are Alice Russell. A dear friend of mine.

Emma And mine.

Lizzie (*smiling*) And Emma's.

The main Lights dim again, leaving Annie in a circle of light. She looks about her

Annie Lizzie?

Nance (*entering the light*) Thank heavens you got here, Alice!

Annie What's this Maggie's been telling me about your father being— killed?

Nance merely points. Annie begins to move towards the couch

Nance It's very ugly.

Annie pauses, then looks. She gasps

Annie (*after a moment*) Who could a' done it?

Nance Father had enemies. We were all sick two days ago. From poison, we think. My stepmother went to Doctor Bowen. He just laughed at her, but was concerned for Father's health, so came to see him.

Henry (*from the darkness, his voice hard*) I refuse to be examined, Bowen. I want no medical attention, and will be most obliged, sir, if you will not call again unless you are summoned! Good morning!

Nance I am so ashamed the way Father treated Doctor Bowen. I was so mortified. But the discourteous way he treated him was nothing unique. He treated lots of folk that way. That is why I think he must a' had a lot of enemies.

Annie Did anyone try to harm him before—before—this?

Nance (*after a pause*) Maybe he caught a burglar in the house? Yes, that may be it. After all, Alice, we've already had two burglaries.

Annie You told me about one. But that was in the barn. About a year ago.

Nance The house was burgled a short while after. Not much stolen. A few trinkets. (*Pause*) Perhaps he came in and saw a burglar—who got scared—and struck out . . .?

Annie With such fury?

Lizzie (*reflectively*) Ten savage blows! Poor Father!

Nance (*echoing*) Poor Father. (*After a pause, softly*) Dead!

Slowly Nance becomes aware that her "father" is dead, and looks into the room once more. With a slight swaying movement she reaches out to Annie, who holds her for a moment before getting a chair and helping her on to it. She then begins fanning Nance, and rubbing her hands

Annie I'll just loosen your dress . . .

Nance It's all right, Alice. I don't feel faint.

Annie I'll get some cologne . . .

Annie moves out of the light, leaving Nance staring ahead of her, stunned. The mood is suddenly shattered by the urgency in Emma's voice

Emma Hush for a moment!

There is the sound of breaking glass, and then a pause. The main Lights go up to reveal Tom standing by the table, a broken wine glass at his feet. Annie is caught in the act of eating a sandwich, whilst being ready to move back into the scene with Nance

Tom I'm sorry—you startled me . . .

Lizzie What is it, Emma?
Emma Listen!

Pause

Lizzie I hear nothing.
Emma I thought I heard something—someone—a prowler . . .
Nance Where?
Emma (*listening*) I'm not sure.
Henry Probably Maggie.
Emma (*impatiently*) Maggie's in the basement. She can't be heard from up here!

Tom stoops to pick up the glass fragments

Lizzie Leave it, Tom. Maggie'll clear it. (*She rings for her, then moves behind Emma, and places a hand on her shoulder*) It's not like you to be so nervous, Emma. You're usually the one . . .
Emma I am not nervous, Lizzie. I most decidedly heard something, and I . . .
Henry Would you like Tom and me to have a look around? To kind of . . .
Lizzie Thank you, but that will be quite unnecessary, Henry. The house is full of creaking old floor-boards, and that, no doubt, is what Emma heard.
Emma I am quite capable of knowing the difference . . .

Maggie enters, interrupting Emma. She looks at Tom approvingly

Tom smiles at Maggie

Lizzie Take the shovel from the fireplace, Maggie, and clean away the broken glass.

Maggie does this, slowly, flirting outrageously with Tom as she stoops at his feet

Annie (*to Nance*) I can quite see why you didn't want me to be Lizzie. I'm in a daze from all these character changes.
Nance You ain't seen nothing yet.

Pause

Henry I'm certainly glad we were able to play this town, Miss Lizzie.
Lizzie I was most excited when I learned you were to visit us.

Pause. Lizzie is waiting for Maggie to go before resuming conversation

Would you like to see my scrapbook cuttings?
Nance I certainly would.

Pause. Lizzie watches Maggie's flirtations with a little impatience

Lizzie Maggie! We do not intend to suspend conversation for the entire evening while you shuffle that glass around. Now, take it away!

With a look of fury Maggie stands up and snaps at Lizzie

Maggie Yes, ma'am!

Maggie sweeps out

Lizzie I'm sorry about that. I'll get the album . . .

Lizzie goes

Nance pulls Tom out of earshot from Emma

Nance Well, Casanova, are you happy at the little scene you created?
Tom Can I help it if I'm completely irresistible?
Nance (*with a sly glance at Annie*) Not completely, Tom. Not completely!

Annie sees the glance, and moves across to them

Tom (*choosing to ignore the reference*) Besides, I was simply being pleasant
   to the girl.
Annie I don't see what business it is of yours, Nance, anyhow.
Nance My! But we're getting bold, aren't we, Annie? Whatever happened
   to the quiet little Annie Beale who crept into this room less than half an
   hour ago? Could it be that her pure, unsullied innocence has been
   besmirched by—that? (*She throws a huge gesture towards the buffet
   table*) By the Demon Punch Bowl?

Pause

Annie I thought you'd never guess!

*Very deliberately, Annie links arms with Tom and leads him to the buffet
table, where she helps herself to some more punch. Provocatively, she
persuades Tom to sip from it. She smiles triumphantly at Nance, whose smile
does not waver*

Nance How romantic! Just like a Viennese operetta!

*With equal deliberation Nance links arms with Henry—much to his astonish-
ment*

   Now, how about dancing a stirring quadrille?

Annie and Nance stare at each other, smiling—but their faces are masks

   Lizzie enters, dusting a large album

Lizzie It may be a little dusty still. I haven't shown it to anyone for a great
   number of years. Emma don't like it.
Emma (*shortly*) Huh! Fat lot you care!

Henry takes the album from Lizzie, and begins glancing through it

Lizzie Now—where was I?
Nance The arrival of the doctor.
Lizzie So I was. (*She laughs*) You've the memory of an elephant, Nance.
Tom Except when it comes to remembering lines.
Henry (*without looking up*) You realize, I take it, that what we are listening
   to is only Lizzie's version of the event?

There is a moment of shocked silence

Emma (*defensively*) Don't you believe her?
Henry That, Miss Emma, is quite beside the point.
Emma I don't see . . .
Lizzie Stop getting angry, Emma. He's right. Of course it's only my version of what happened.
Henry I just didn't want anyone to lose sight of this. What Lizzie tells you is not, of necessity, fact, but the story that got a jury to acquit her.
Annie Henry! That's rude!
Nance Forgive him, Lizzie. It's this morbid preoccupation with truth that he has. It makes him . . .
Henry I'm not saying that I don't believe it . . .
Annie I should hope not. It's . . .
Henry But, on the other hand, I'd rather weigh the facts first.
Lizzie (*smiling*) The "facts" as I present them? How do you know them to be "facts", Henry? They could be very ingenious half-truths—or even downright lies, couldn't they? (*To the company at large*) However, it wasn't my "story"—as Henry puts it—that got me acquitted.
Emma (*sharply*) It was her innocence.
Lizzie No, not even that, dear Emma. It was the muddle of the affair that really acquitted me. The police botched the whole business from beginning to end. (*She turns, smiling, to Nance*) And now, to pick up at the doctor's entrance . . .

The Lights dim and the spot comes up as before. Nance seats herself on the chair in the circle of light and begins to take up the scene from the point at which Emma spoke, and Tom dropped the glass, but she is again interrupted— this time by Annie

Annie (*in a loud whisper*) Who am I now?
Nance (*with exaggerated patience*) Mrs Churchill, dear. But you're not on yet.

Nance takes the pose, and, after a moment, Henry enters the light

Henry Drink this, Lizzie. It's a sedative. Is there anything else I can do for you?
Nance Emma's at Fairhaven. Would you be so kind as to go to the telegraph office and send her a wire?
Henry Most certainly I will.
Nance Put it as gently as you can because there is an old person there and the shock might be too much for her.
Henry I understand. Mrs Churchill will . . . (*He looks about him, then repeats loudly*) Mrs Churchill will . . . Where on earth is . . .

Annie enters the area, her mouth filled with sandwich

Annie (*almost unintelligible*) Yes, Doctor?
Henry By all means finish your meal before we continue. (*To Nance, after a slight pause*) Mrs Churchill will take care of you. Eventually. (*He goes*)

Annie He's a fine man, is Doctor Bowen. (*Pause*) But where's your step-mother all this time?

Nance She went to visit someone who is sick.

Annie Anyone I know?

Nance She didn't say. She received a note. (*Pause. Tiredly*) I don't know but she is killed, too, for I thought I heard her come in.

Annie Shall I look, dear?

Nance (*nodding*) I think we should. Get Maggie to help.

Annie goes off. Nance sits staring ahead for a moment, then puts her hands to her eyes and tries peering outside the circle of light at Lizzie

Hey! Lizzie!

Lizzie What is it?

Nance So far, you haven't mentioned there was someone else staying at the house. Why? Is he the one you suspect?

Tom Who's she yapping about?

Lizzie Uncle John Vinnicum Morse.

Emma Brother to our real mother.

Tom Did he live with you?

Lizzie No. He'd simply stayed overnight—the night before the killings.

Tom Didn't that strike anyone as being a little—odd?

Emma Why should it? He often stayed overnight.

Lizzie Hush, Emma. Of course it struck folk as odd. In fact, downright peculiar. Particularly in view of his being a horse-trader. They didn't like horse-traders any more then than they like 'em now, and they'd a' lynched him, could they but have layed hands on him.

Tom Was he around that morning?

Lizzie He'd gone to see a friend across town.

Nance gets back into character as Henry enters the circle of light

Nance Did you send the wire to Emma, Doctor?

Henry (*nodding*) I worded it most carefully. (*He looks around for Annie*)

Nance Mrs Churchill's upstairs . . .

Nance is interrupted by the slow entrance of Annie, whose face shows that Mrs Borden, too, is dead

Nance (*softly*) Is there another?

Annie Yes, she is up there.

Henry "goes off" quickly to examine the body

Maggie saw her first. As we reached the top of the stairs, with our eyes at the level of the bedroom floor, she looked across through the open door . . . (*She pauses for a moment, visualizing the scene*) There, on the other side of the room—beyond the bed—we could just see her. Maggie pointed her out to me . . .

Nance rises from the chair

No! Don't go to her, Lizzie!

However, Nance gives the chair to Annie, who allows herself to be helped on to it

We went into the room. (*Impulsively*) It's the work of a madman!

Pause

Nance Is the room disturbed?

Annie No. I don't think it could have been robbery.

Nance puts her hands on Annie's shoulders for a moment

Nance I don't know what I'd have done without you, Mrs Churchill.

Lizzie (*tonelessly*) Nineteen blows!

Annie A madman!

Lizzie (*incredulously*) Nineteen! (*Pause*) She died an hour or so before my father.

Emma The medical examiner said she died between nine and ten.

Lizzie Maggie, the maid . . .

Annie Maggie?

Lizzie (*laughing*) Heavens, Annie, not this one. She'd have been a mere child at the time of the event. No, the maid we had at the time—also called Maggie—stated that she'd seen Abbie alive at nine thirty. So that would put her death between nine-thirty and ten o'clock.

Tom enters the circle of light

Tom I'm Special Officer Harrington, ma'am, and I'd like to ask a few questions.

Annie It's been a bitter experience for her, and . . .

Tom I appreciate that, ma'am, but we must know what happened. (*He pauses, and looks at Nance for a moment*) On the other hand, owing to the atrociousness of this crime perhaps you are not in a mental condition to give as clear a statement of the facts as you will be tomorrow.

Nance (*calmly*) No, I can tell you all I know just as well now as at any other time.

Tom looks at her, suspiciously

Emma He took her calmness as a sign of guilt. The man was a fool!

Lizzie But, Emma, you weren't even there.

Emma Mrs Churchill told me. Besides, fancy suspecting you!

Tom (*to Nance*) The time of your father's death is placed at a little after eleven a.m. Where were you at that time?

Nance Out back, in the barn. I went there about a quarter to, I guess. I was up in the loft looking for some pieces of lead, to cut into sinkers.

Tom Sinkers?

Nance That is what I said, officer.

Tom For fishing?

Nance (*surprised*) What else?

Tom I'm only trying to establish a fact, Miss Borden. You intended to go fishing?

Nance I had plans for visiting some friends at Marion next Monday.
Tom I see. (*He makes notes on an imaginary pad*) How long would you say you stayed in the barn?
Nance (*after a pause*) About twenty minutes—half an hour . . .

Tom makes more notes

Tom Your father—had he any enemies you know of?
Nance I imagine there were a few . . .
Tom But you know nothing more specific than that?
Nance (*after deliberation*) No . . .
Emma (*suddenly*) What about Joseph W. Carpenter?
Lizzie You can't be serious?
Tom Who was Joseph W. Carpenter?
Lizzie He stole from my father, who, as you probably know, was a mortician . . .

A spot comes up on Henry, who talks to an imaginary Mr Borden

Henry All right, Mr Borden, so I embezzled six thousand dollars from you. I needed the money. Who don't? But you're not going to see me go to prison for it, are you? (*He listens*) Well, I can think of several reasons why not. For instance, suppose people was to discover how the expensive coffins you was selling 'em was not the same boxes as was lowered into the earth containing their loved ones? (*He laughs*) They might think it sacrilegious—to say nothin' of it being a swindle. (*Pause*) So why don't we be sensible? Look, I've got about three thousand dollars-worth of property. This I'll make over to you, and I'll raise what else I can from my friends. How's that? (*He listens*) I knew you'd see the light. After all, if I went to prison you'd get nothing. And think of the publicity! Always remember—an undertaker's reputation can mean life or death to him, Mr Borden!

Henry laughs at this as the spot fades on him. As his laughter dies out that of Lizzie is heard

Lizzie That's outrageous exaggeration, Henry!
Emma Carpenter was an unpleasant man. They say he never forgave Father for taking everything he had. And don't forget he was seen in Fall River about the day of the killings.
Lizzie Maybe he was, maybe he wasn't. Folk were prepared to believe anything at the time. They were scared. There was panic. Two people had been savagely slain, in broad daylight. Men were worried about their families.
Henry (*from the darkness*) Well, I for one, don't aim to go back to the mill this afternoon! I wanna be where I can keep an eye on Ruthie and the kids till this maniac's locked up where he belongs!
Emma Most of the mills were forced to shut down for the afternoon because so few of the workers returned after their lunch . . .
Lizzie Though I never quite understood how they planned to defend their families, whilst propping up the bars in the local saloons!

Nance and Tom are still in the circle of light, with Annie

Tom But don't you remember his life being actually threatened, ever? (*Pause*) Maybe you thought it a joke at the time—or didn't take it seriously?

Nance thinks for a moment

Nance No. Though there was the poison . . . At least, we thought it to be poison. All of us were sick, including him . . .

Nance goes on explaining this, and Tom continues to take notes during the following conversation

Emma Harrington hated Lizzie, right from the start. He was convinced she did it.

Lizzie You could hardly blame him for that. The evidence did begin to pile up.

Emma Circumstantial evidence. He had a hand in that, too.

Tom makes the gesture of putting the note-book in his pocket

Tom Well, I guess that's all for now, Miss Borden. We'll put a check on the drug stores to see if they come up with anything. If anyone did try to obtain poison recently he'd have been forced to sign the poison register, so he'll be on record. Good day to you, ma'am. (*He moves into the darkness*)

Nance looks at Annie

Nance You know what, Mrs Churchill? Special Officer Harrington thinks I did it. (*Pause*) It's not a very flattering thought, is it?

As the light dims slowly on them, Emma's voice is heard

Emma He didn't aim to leave no stone unturned in his persecution a' Lizzie. And he got the sort of slander he was looking for in the D. R. Smith Pharmacy on the corner of Columbia Street and South Main— from the drug-store clerk, Eli Bence . . .

A spot goes up on another area, lighting Henry. Tom enters the area

Henry Hi there, Mr Harrington. D'you think there'll be an arrest soon? No-one's gonna sleep until there is, you know. Gee! I never thought I'd see such excitement in this town! But what can I get you?

Tom I'm just making official enquiries, Eli. About poison.

Henry You want to see the poison book?

Tom Yeah. Just a formality.

Henry goes through the motions of presenting Lizzie's scrapbook as the register, and Tom turns pages, studying them. He speaks without looking up

These names represent everyone who's been in here to purchase poison over—say—the last month . . . ?

Henry That's right, Mr Harrington. At least, those are the names of the people who actually purchased poison.

Tom I don't follow . . . ?

Henry Well, some folk don't care much for signing that book. I guess they've their reasons. For instance. Two days ago a young woman came by, asking for ten cents' worth of prussic acid. Naturally, I told her she'd need a doctor's prescription, so she went away.

Tom Did she mention why she wanted it?

Henry To kill moths in a fur garment, she said.

Tom That don't sound right. Is prussic acid used for such a purpose?

Henry Search me. Anyhow, she had this fur cape over her arm, and that's the reason she gave for wanting the poison.

Tom Did you know her?

Henry No.

Tom Would you recognize her if you saw her again?

Henry Oh yes, Mr Harrington. I'd certainly recognize her.

Tom Good. (*He thinks on this*) Say, would you meet me this evening, after the store closes? You may be able to help. I won't keep you long.

Henry Sure thing! Anything to help out.

Tom How about—nine-thirty?

Henry Certainly, Mr Harrington.

Tom On the corner of Second Street.

Henry I'll be there.

The light fades. The half-hour chimes and a light goes up on another area. Tom enters, followed by Henry

Tom You wait over there, out of sight.

Henry moves out of the light. Tom goes through the motions of knocking at a door

Nance (*from the darkness*) Maggie! See who's knocking at the door.

Annie (*from the darkness in an Irish accent*) I'm going, Miss Lizzie.

Sour-faced, Annie enters the light and "opens the door"

Tom I'd like to see Miss Lizzie Borden.

Annie I'll see if she's at home to you. (*She goes into the darkness. Her voice is heard*) It's Special Officer Harrington.

Nance Ask him in.

Annie moves back into the light

Annie She says for you to come on in.

Tom Tell her I'd rather see her here, if it's all the same with her. I won't bother to come in.

Annie (*mumbling as she goes into the darkness*) Running a poor girl off her feet, and after the ordeal I've suffered! He says he'd rather see you at the door, if it's all the same with you. (*Softly*) And if it's all the same with you I wish you'd make up your mind, to save me poor ol' feet.

Nance (*puzzled*) All right, Maggie. I'll go see him.

Nance appears in the circle of light

Yes?

Tom I'm sorry to bother you, Miss Borden, but there's been talk of a man prowling about in the yard. Have you noticed anything suspicious?

Nance No.

Tom I just looked around, and everything certainly seems all right. You'll contact us if you do see anything, won't you?

Nance (*looking a little puzzled*) Of course, Officer.

Tom (*at a loss for words*) Fine. Yes. Fine. Then I'll be off. Good night, ma'am.

Nance Good night.

Nance "shuts the door", and goes off into the darkness. Henry joins Tom in the circle of light

Tom Well?

Henry That was her! She was the one who asked for the prussic acid.

Tom Are you sure of that?

Henry As sure as I stand here.

Tom (*smiling triumphantly*) I had a hunch it'd be her!

Henry (*excitedly*) That was Lizzie Borden, wasn't it?

Tom (*still smiling*) Yes, Eli. That was Lizzie Borden.

The light fades

Lizzie (*smiling*) A real sneaky one, was Special Officer Harrington.

Nance You've already told us you were suspected at the onset, Lizzie, but you didn't say what motive they attributed to you.

Lizzie Take your choice. They were various . . .

Emma Mean and cruel, every one!

The light comes up on Annie, Nance, Tom and Henry as a group of gossips

Nance (*in a conspiratorial whisper*) I did hear tell that Mr and Mrs Chase visited the house the very night before the killings. And do you know what they heard?

Annie (*excitedly*) Do tell!

Nance A quarrel!

A significant pause ensues as they look at each other. Tom whistles his amazement

Henry Who was quarrelling?

Nance She was. With her father.

Annie Did they hear what it was about?

Nance (*after a dramatic pause*) They heard him say, "I will know the name of the man who got you into trouble!"

Shocked silence. Annie is the first to recover

Annie Doesn't surprise me one little bit. She looks the type. Come to think of it, she's been putting on a little weight lately. Haven't any of you noticed it?

Tom I heard she killed the old man to stop him from altering his will. There must be at least a quarter of a million dollars at stake.

Henry You could be right, though I heard tell somewhere as to how there was a difference of opinion over a property deal some years ago, and Lizzie threatened to kill him.

Emma (*involuntarily*) That's a lie!

The spot fades on the gossips and the main Lights come up

Lizzie There had been a difference of opinion on a property deal. Though it happened a good five years before the slayings.

Emma You make it sound worse than it was ...

Lizzie There was ill feeling.

Emma We both felt the same, Lizzie and me. (*To Lizzie*) But you didn't threaten to kill him, no more than I did.

Lizzie You shouldn't take gossips so seriously, Emma. Ignore 'em. That's the way to make 'em wither in the sun. (*To Nance*) It's a little complicated, I'm afraid, but you ought to know about it, because it was considered a very possible motive—or, at least, a sparking point. You see, Abby had a stepmother and stepsister, and when Abby's father died he left them a small house to share.

Emma Just the stepmother, and stepsister, you understand?

Lizzie Well, at first things went fine, but there came a day when the widow needed some cash ...

Emma Huh! No-one ever knew what she needed it for. It was a trick!

Lizzie That is of no importance, Emma. The fact is, that she needed some ready money, so wanted to sell her half of the property. Unfortunately, the stepsister—who was married, incidentally, to a man who wasn't doing very well—couldn't afford to buy her mother's half, which meant the house would have to go up for sale. This, in turn, meant that if the new owner wanted the house for himself, Abby's stepsister and husband would be forced to leave.

Emma However, the situation never arose, because Abby intervened, and Father bought the widow's half, handing the title of the property over to Abby. Which is probably what she had in mind in the first place!

Lizzie He foolishly kept the transaction secret from Emma and me.

Emma And whose idea do you suppose that was?

Lizzie Naturally there were a few well-meaning neighbours in the town who felt sure we knew already, but, nevertheless, felt it their duty to mention it in passing ...

Emma Fifteen hundred dollars he'd paid for it! And handed over the title to Abby, on a silver platter!

Lizzie I've no doubt she meant well ...

Emma For her own side of the family!

Lizzie Naturally, Emma and I confronted him with it, and told him what he did for her family he ought to do for his own children.

Emma (*smugly*) So he did for us what he'd done for her.

Lizzie Exactly the same. Gave each of us title to property valued at fifteen hundred dollars.

Nance D'ya mean to say they took the business of the house and all that seriously, as a motive?

Lizzie (*shrugging her shoulders*) Why not? It was a time of panic—of desperation. Try to realize the atmosphere in the town. They needed a killer. Someone behind bars, just so everyone could feel safe—and sleep. You see, even though I wasn't exactly behind bars, so long as they could produce gossip that pointed to my guilt they felt safe—convincing themselves it was me. That way, they knew whom to watch.

Emma The story was already circulating town that Lizzie had tried obtaining prussic acid from Eli Bence, and now other witnesses mysteriously appeared to support his tale!

Lizzie And straight on top of that came the business of the barn.

Annie What "business of the barn"?

Emma People ready to swear she'd not been near it that morning.

Annie (*surprised*) Is that so?

Lizzie Don't you see, that I couldn't have killed Father if I'd been in the barn at the time I said. And, since it was automatically assumed that both killings were by the same hand, it meant I couldn't have killed my stepmother, neither. So, if they wanted to prove me guilty, they had first to prove that I was lying about going into the barn.

Emma A patrolman, William H. Medley offered evidence . . .

The stage darkens, leaving only a circle of light focussed on Tom and Henry

Henry Do you realize the importance of this testimony, Medley?

Tom Yes, sir.

Henry And you're sure?

Tom Sure I'm sure.

Henry It's certainly the break we've been looking for . . .

Tom I figured that.

Henry Her story sounded unlikely, from the start.

Tom That's just what I thought, so . . .

Henry On the other hand, of course, it's crazy enough to be true.

Tom You think so?

Henry Well—not after what you just told me, obviously. But, until then, I had one or two doubts regarding her guilt . . .

Tom I was never in doubt. That's why, the minute I heard she'd been up in the barn-loft looking for lead I planned sashaying out there and taking a peek for myself.

Henry What did you expect to find?

Tom I don't know. Maybe nothing. Maybe fresh clues . . . (*After a moment's pause*) She was too damn calm.

Henry (*pause—then reflectively*) My wife never cries. Not even when our boy was drowned. She went on long walks. But she never cried.

Tom is not particularly interested in this revelation, but more concerned with his own achievement

Tom When I climbed the steps to the loft, I noticed something—odd. At first I couldn't figure what it was, but after I put my hands on the loft floor, to help myself up, I realized. It was thick with dust, and my hands had left an imprint. (*After a pause*) The only imprint. If she'd a' been there, there'd a' been footmarks, wouldn't there?

Henry There were no other marks on the loft floor at all?
Tom Only those made by me.
Henry And you're prepared to testify that in the courthouse, if necessary?
Tom You bet I am!

The spot dims: the main Lights come up

Emma He could hardly wait. They all had it in for Lizzie. Everything she said they labelled a lie. Folk were real mean to her. Especially the police.
Lizzie It happened on the day of the policemen's annual outing. I guess they figured I was taking advantage of their absence.
Annie (*thoughtfully*) I still don't quite see why it was important that you establish so precisely at what time you were in the barn.
Lizzie The killing of my father took place around eleven a.m. and the police were notified about a quarter after. I would have needed to be in the house all that time to have hidden the weapon, washed myself down, changed my dress—which would have been saturated with blood, hidden my clothing . . . (*She pauses, then laughs*) There were, of course, theories as to how I solved that little problem—of the blood . . .

The Lights fade to a spot on Nance and Henry

Nance I just happened to be passing the house, and I just happened to glance up at this window, and there she was—her hair and ears covered in a rubber cap! (*Pause*) I thought nothing of it at the time—I mean, who would? (*Pause*) A rubber cap!
Henry A friend of mine reckons he saw her standing at the window, with a hatchet in her hand, watching for her father to arrive. (*Pause*) And he says she was as naked as a new-born babe!
Nance I saw this with my own eyes. (*Pause*) I simply am not able to understand why they have not gone right on in there and arrested her!
Henry Everybody knows she did it. How can the police be so blind?

Nance shakes her head in complete astonishment. The spot dims and the main Lights come up

Lizzie The police were following up various clues . . .
Emma Lizzie and me tried to help them. We advertized in the newspaper, offering a five thousand dollar reward to anyone who could give information leading to the arrest of the killer.
Lizzie But they were too busy trying to prove there'd been no note.
Annie Note? What note?
Nance Why do we always have to go back twenty pages, to remind you of the plot?
Lizzie On the morning of the crimes Mrs Borden had told me she'd gotten a note and was going out on a sick call. Naturally, I told this to the Sheriff's Office, and they began a search for the note.
Annie Did she visit someone?
Lizzie How should I know? I didn't hear her go out, but I thought I heard her come in . . . (*Pause*) There was never another opportunity to talk to her.

Emma Just because they never found the note, they said Lizzie was lying. It's my guess Abby burned it. Why should she hang on to a note, once she'd read it?

Henry (*thoughtfully*) It's equally possible that no such note existed.

Annie Henry!

Nance Some day he's going to discover that truth's a bottomless pit. Whilst he's falling in it, as like as not.

Lizzie Why shouldn't he have doubts? After all, it's only my version you're hearing. I could be the world's number one liar. In fact, maybe Henry has it already figured out why I should lie about such a note?

Henry Well—yes.

Nance Oh, he's real smart. Not just a nondescript actor!

Lizzie Go on, Henry . . .

Henry You'd told the maid that Mrs Borden was out on a sick call?

Lizzie That's right.

Henry It was to explain why she wasn't moving about the house.

Lizzie In other words . . . ?

Henry Of course, this is only theory . . .

Emma Slander, more likely!

Lizzie You think it was an excuse to keep Maggie's curiosity dormant whilst I figured out a way to deal with the—the awkward situation of— of explaining away the body?

Henry Something like that.

Emma If only you'd go to the police, Lizzie, and tell them whom you suspect, it would stop such—such foul slanders.

Nance Emma's right, of course, but . . .

Henry But Lizzie enjoys being an enigma! Let's face it.

Pause—then Lizzie laughs

Lizzie He's ruthless, isn't he?

Henry (*smiling*) Go on, Lizzie. Deny it.

Slight pause

Lizzie That I required time to explain the body? Or that I enjoy being an enigma?

Henry (*challengingly*) Either!

They stare at each other, both amused by the situation. Annie, who does not understand, feels the need to break the silence

Annie Where's your manners, Henry?

Lizzie It's not a question of manners, Annie . . .

Nance (*wrily, in a loud whisper*) It's a question of truth, dear heart.

Lizzie (*equally wrily*) That's right. As Nance says, in her own inimitable, subtle fashion—it's a question of truth.

Nance raises her eyebrows at Lizzie, usurping her own style, but there is no animosity

Nance (*smiling*) Someday I must allow you to portray me on the stage.

Lizzie Someday someone must allow you to portray yourself on the stage. (*To Henry*) It's good to find someone with doubts. I'm sick to death of people smiling as they talk to me, pretending to believe I didn't do it, without asking a single—awkward—embarrassing question. Yet they think I did it. As sure as God made little green apples, they believe it, and nothing on this earth will ever persuade them to the contrary. So you go ahead and doubt, Henry Webb.

Henry It would account for there being no footsteps in the barn . . .

Lizzie Agreed.

Henry Since you'd a' lied about that, too.

Nance Sherlock Holmes has gone to his head.

Henry (*ignoring her*) As for the poison . . .

Nance Ah but she didn't obtain the poison. Eli Bence didn't serve her.

Henry Some other pharmacist may have been a mite less scrupulous.

Lizzie (*deliberately setting up the skittles for him*) But I suffered from the poisoning, too.

Henry Elementary, my dear Watson. A clever move to divert suspicion. You took a little yourself.

Tom Even were your ideas correct, Henry, I'd hardly consider them sufficient evidence for putting a person on trial for their life.

Henry points to the scrapbook

Henry But there were other factors, Tom. Factors she hasn't mentioned— by design—by accident—but they've not been mentioned. The dress, for instance . . .

Henry stares at Lizzie. She holds his stare for a moment, then turns to Tom, and laughs

Lizzie There's no escaping his vengeance, is there?

Tom What about the dress?

Lizzie It all centred around the search for bloodstains . . .

The Lights dim to a spot on Nance and Annie

Annie Lizzie . . .

Nance What is it, Alice?

Annie (*aside*) I'm Alice Russell.

Tom Congratulations on your brilliant characterization!

Nance You look troubled, Alice.

Annie That dress—the one I saw you burning yesterday . . .

Nance Oh, that old thing! It was covered with paint. I'd told myself a hundred times I ought to burn it, but . . .

Annie I am afraid, Lizzie, the worst thing you could have done was to burn that dress. I have been asked about your dresses.

Nance (*after a pause*) Asked about them?

Annie nods

Oh, what made you let me do it? Why didn't you stop me?

A pause

Annie They asked me again today, and—and . . .

Nance (*calmly*) You told them you saw me burning it?

Annie (*almost in tears*) I didn't mean no harm to you Lizzie. But it's the truth, isn't it? You did burn it.

Nance I just didn't think, Alice. I just didn't think.

Annie moves out of the light, leaving Nance alone, thoughtfully staring out into space, whilst Lizzie's voice is heard

Lizzie For a week plans had been under discussion for my arrest. Once I asked Mayor Coughlin if anyone in the house was suspected. He tried to evade answering, but I was firm. So, eventually, he was forced to answer . . .

Henry (*from the darkness*) Well, Miss Borden, I regret to answer, but I must answer you. Yes, you are suspected.

During the following speech Tom and Henry enter the circle of light and silently make the formal arrest

Lizzie So, finally, on August eleventh, exactly one week after the murders, came the arrest. Even though I'd known it was me they were building a case against, it still came as a horrible shock. Not because my life was at stake—in fact, I didn't think about that—but because they could believe me capable of such a crime. I'd lived among them, talked to them—was just another neighbour . . . Then, suddenly, they were able to see me as some kind of—of monster!

Nance buries her head in her hands, but briefly. Tom places a hand on her shoulder. She composes herself before speaking

Nance I am ready to go now.

Nance moves into the darkness with Tom and Henry. Emma's voice is heard. As she speaks, the main Lights come up

Emma It's no good, Lizzie. Your stories about creaking floorboards do not console me. There is, most decidedly, a prowler.

Lizzie For heaven's sake, Emma, what exactly is it you heard?

Emma (*listening*) It made my blood run cold. It was someone—laughing. A most eerie sound. (*She shudders*) There! There it was again! (*She looks around, but no one else has heard it*) I'm not a fool, Lizzie! It is not my imagination!

Henry Maybe it'd be better if Tom and I were to—look around a bit?

Lizzie Oh, please don't . . .

Emma I'd appreciate that, Mr Webb. Really appreciate it. Thank you. (*She glares at Lizzie*) I do not understand why you seem so surprised. After all, you did say you thought you were followed home!

Tom and Henry leave to investigate as—

the CURTAIN *falls*

ACT II

The same. Half an hour later

As the CURTAIN *rises Emma is playing the piano, finishing a somewhat embellished arrangement of "The Last Rose of Summer". Lizzie, Tom and Annie are grouped at the piano. Annie occasionally throws a furtive glance towards Nance and Henry, who sit some distance away, whispering furiously. The music stops and Tom applauds. Nance and Henry look across*

Nance That was lovely, dear.

Emma (*shyly*) Lizzie plays much better, really . . .

Lizzie Nonsense, Emma. The music I play is a little more elevated, but I don't play it half as well. Poor Mr Chopin must spin in his grave!

Emma Lizzie! That's no way to talk of the dead.

Tom Please play some more, Miss Emma.

Emma Oh, but I . . .

Annie (*enthusiastically*) Please do!

Emma Well, I'd need to sort out something . . .

Annie Play "The Last Rose of Summer" again.

Emma Would you really like that?

Annie nods

Tom We'd love you to.

Emma begins to play, so Nance and Henry continue their conversation

Nance Come on, Henry, tell me. Tell Auntie Nance. Why do you prefer not to notice Annie's infatuation for you?

Henry What a meddlesome ol' romantic you are, Nance. D'you know that? And, if you want Uncle Henry's sound advice—

Nance Which I don't . . .

Henry —you'd give up the theatre, and open up a Matrimonial Bureau. Nance O'Neil's Matchmaking Agency. In lights! I can see . . .

Nance (*coolly*) You're evading the issue, Henry.

Henry (*after a pause*) She'll get over it.

Nance Why don't you respond?

Henry (*smiles*) Trifle with her affections?

Nance She'd love it.

Henry Correction. You'd love it.

Nance Fair comment. Just consider the situation, Henry. We have a classical farce in progress. I am interested in Tom, who is interested in Annie, who, in turn, is interested in Henry. And who is no-one interested in? You've guessed. The fabulous, lovable, Nance O'Neil. Naturally, it would be to my advantage if you responded to Annie. That way, Tom'd get cold feet, and what better place to warm them than . . .

Henry The fabulous, lovable, Nance O'Neil?
Nance Say that as though you mean it.

Pause

Henry It wouldn't work.
Nance Why not? Tom and I had our—moments—in the past.
Henry (*shrugging his shoulders*) I couldn't do it.
Nance Oh? For what reason?

Pause. Henry laughs, somewhat uneasily

Henry I'm an actor, not a great lover.
Nance (*smiling*) The two are usually synonymous. But you're being evasive again, aren't you? (*Pause*) Where's—the truth—Henry?

Pause

Don't you ever feel the need for—affection?
Henry Is it affection we're talking of? Or lust?
Nance A little healthy lust never did anyone any harm. Doesn't your lack of—desire for relationships—ever strike you as being—well—unnatural?
Henry It obviously strikes you as being so.
Nance Perhaps odd, rather than unnatural. Not that I'm suggesting anything, you understand?
Henry Aren't you? Pardon my mistrust of you, Nance, but here was I, sitting thinking it was only a matter of time before you presented me with a big fat "home truth"!
Nance (*laughing*) I was merely generalizing. After all, the theatre's full of odd people. I remember well that blonde young man in the tour we . . .
Henry I remember it well, too. You've related it at least a thousand times.
Nance But I had to tear my dress from his back, Henry! Going to a party, indeed! I shudder to think a' the doings that went on that night!

Pause

But not in my dress with the emerald spangles!

Pause

Such a nice boy, too. He was . . .
Henry Is there some particular point in regaling me with this very boring story yet once again, Nance?

Pause

Nance I guess not. Well, if you insist on not noticing Annie, I guess Tom will continue looking in her direction . . . You're not afraid you'd fail her, are you?

The music stops

Henry Meaning . . . ?
Nance (*shrugging*) Ah, the pity of it all. None of us will get the opportunity to discover our real selves, will we?

Annie joins Henry and Nance

Tom You sure are talented, Miss Emma. If ever you decide you'd like a job in the theatre . . . (*He laughs*)

Emma is flattered

Emma You should hear Lizzie.

Lizzie (*to Tom*) She always insists I do everything better, but it is simply not true.

Annie (*to Nance and Henry*) Don't you know it's rude to whisper in company?

Nance Depends on what you're whispering about, dear. Sometimes it's a heap ruder to say it aloud. (*She laughs*)

Annie (*irritated*) You know what I mean!

Nance I prefer to misconstrue you, sweetie.

Lizzie (*calling to them*) Has everyone had sufficient cookies and coffee?

They all nod, or state they have had sufficient

Then I'll ring for Maggie to clear the wreckage. (*She does so*) I'm quite sure you've all had more than sufficient music for one evening.

Lizzie smiles at Emma, who is not amused, and slams down the lid of the piano, flounces to her chair, and grimly attacks her embroidery

I meant no harm, Emma . . .

Emma It's sheer carelessness, Lizzie! You say these things—not caring how people feel. I was . . .

Maggie enters, interrupting Emma

Lizzie Take the coffee things, Maggie.

As Maggie does this, Lizzie holds a formal conversation, addressing Nance

It always amazes me how actresses are able to become other people . . . Is it so difficult, Nance?

Nance I never become anyone else. My ego would never allow it.

Lizzie But you seem to become—well, whoever you're playing.

Nance It's a box of tricks, Lizzie.

Tom Many of them even older than Nance.

Maggie hovers near Tom, and slows down in order to attract his attention

Nance I simulate reality. I do not attempt to be reality. God! That I should shoot myself every time we play *Hedda Gabler*!

Henry What a tempting thought.

Lizzie Maggie! We haven't all night!

Maggie casts a look of fury at Lizzie, and speeds up her collection of the cups, etc.

Nance How can you expect an actress to actually believe herself to be Gertrude, the mother of this fool of a boy, Hamlet, who mopes around, shedding tears like they're going out of style? I mean, any good American mother, in her right mind, would have packed her bags and got out of that castle the minute she realized there was something rotten in the state of Denmark! (*She laughs*)

Maggie finishes collecting the débris, and after brilliantly smiling at Tom, goes toward the door. She is stopped by Lizzie's voice

Lizzie By the way, Maggie, have you been outside, in the garden, today?
Maggie No, ma'am.
Lizzie You're quite sure?
Maggie Do you not believe me?
Lizzie That'll be all.
Maggie If you don't . . .
Lizzie I said that'll be all, Maggie!

Maggie goes

Tom So they weren't Maggie's footprints outside the window?
Emma I knew there was someone lurking about.
Annie Why should anyone be interested in spying on us?
Nance Why should anyone be interested in following Lizzie home?
Emma You just don't think, Lizzie. You should have gone to the police, and told them your suspicions. I'm just as much in danger as you are. I don't know why I go on living here with you. I'd no doubt be far happier alone.
Lizzie Stop it, Emma! Show consideration for our guests.
Emma Your guests, Lizzie. Not mine.
Lizzie (*to Nance*) I'm sorry, Nance. We have these little domestic scenes occasionally . . .
Emma Occasionally? Huh!
Lizzie (*turning on her*) All right, Emma. We have them frequently. And each time you threaten to leave. But that's no reason for boring our— my—guests with our petty quarrelling!

An awkward pause, during which Emma furiously and deliberately stabs at her embroidery. Nance comes to the rescue

Nance Well, anyway, he's gone now, whoever it was. So go on telling us about the trial, Lizzie. I'm dying to know what went on after the arrest.

The main Lights dim to a spot during the following

Lizzie (*reflectively*) The arrest . . . (*She pauses, contemplating for a moment*) The period between the arrest and the trial saw more—speculation—and foolishness—than any other similar event in history, I imagine.

Pause. Annie moves into the spot

Like the chatter of that ol' biddy, Hannah Reagon . . .
Emma She was the matron at the gaol.
Lizzie And the town's biggest gossip, to boot.
Annie (*talking to an imaginary reporter*) So you're Edwin Porter, from the *Fall River Globe*? Well, I most certainly am glad you came, since I do think folk in Fall River should know about this conversation I heard

between Lizzie and her sister, Emma, down at the courthouse. As near to a confession as makes no difference. (*Pause. A trifle sharply*) Don't rush me, Mr Porter! (*Pause*) Well, as I told you before, Emma is in the habit of visiting her sister every morning, and normally I pay no heed. Why should I? Just sisterly chat—about the family, and so forth. What's left of it, that is! (*She laughs*) But this morning . . . (*She shakes her head, marvelling at the enormity of what she heard*) Mind you, it's not in my nature to listen to the conversation of others. After all, that's eavesdropping, isn't it? But this morning, during Emma's visit, I was—now, where was I? Don't hurry me. That way, I'll never remember. I've got it. I was cleaning the room next door, when I heard their voices raised in anger. Naturally, I was concerned. If she killed her parents, there's no telling what Lizzie might do to her sister, is there? Anyhow, so I listened. And I heard her say, "Emma, you have given me away, haven't you?" (*She pauses for dramatic effect*) And Emma replied, "No, Lizzie. I have not." But Lizzie was not a bit satisfied, and told her, "You have, and I will let you see I won't give in one inch."
Emma She was lying!
Annie (*to the imaginary reporter*) And they just glared at one another.

The spot fades on her and the main Lights come up

Emma Lying! She was proved a liar at the trial. She admitted to it being a lie.
Annie But why should she do such a thing?
Nance For a round of applause, dear heart. There are heaps of folk like that, even outside showbiz. I once knew a woman . . .
Tom Whatever the situation, Nance always knew a woman!
Henry It's her ploy for getting a round of applause.

Pause, then Nance laughs

Nance What chance have I here, with you two upstaging me?
Emma (*obstinately*) It was libel. We should a' sued.
Lizzie They did me less harm than they did the prosecution.
Annie (*excitedly*) But what about the trial?
Lizzie (*thoughtfully*) Yes—the trial . . .

The Lights fade to a spot. Henry moves into it. He adopts a pose, and appears ready to embark upon his speech. Lizzie looks across and laughs

Of course, in actual fact, Henry, you don't look the tiniest bit like the prosecuting counsel.

Henry frowns

Nance Oh dear, now you've totally ruined his characterization. He'll be floating about like a piece of driftwood, in search of some kind of shore.
Lizzie (*contritely*) I'm sorry . . .
Nance Fill him in with a few clues, honey. (*In a loud whisper*) Fictitious ones, if necessary.
Lizzie Well, there's little to say, really . . . Oh, I've got it! His coat-tails!

Nance His coat-tails?
Lizzie He toyed with them—depending upon his mood. Sometimes twisting them—rolling them into a ball—pulling them apart—tying them . . .

Henry tries this

How's that, Henry?

Pause

Henry A tiny bit theatrical, don't you think?
Nance Oh? I felt it rather your style.

Henry begins trying out various rather dramatic voices, his back to the audience as he addresses the jury upstage

Henry Gentlemen of the jury . . . Gentlemen of the jury . . . Gentlemen of the . . .
Lizzie (*softly*) He was very quietly spoken . . .

Henry turns, and is about to explode, but Lizzie quickly forestalls him

Knowing you to be such a stickler for truth, I just thought I ought to mention it.

Henry contains himself, and works himself into character

Henry Gentlemen of the jury . . . (*He waits for a further interruption from Lizzie. Since none is forthcoming, he decides to continue*) It is my firm intention to prove to you, beyond the vestige of doubt, that the prisoner, Lizzie Borden, did murder both her father and her stepmother in a most brutal and callous fashion on August fourth . . . (*He turns upstage and silently addresses the jury during Lizzie's conversation. He turns downstage whenever he speaks*)
Lizzie For ninety minutes he talked . . .
Henry I will illustrate the animosity that existed in the family over a property deal . . .
Lizzie Everyone in the courthouse was watching me. Like vultures. Steely, unfeeling eyes. I don't know what they expected. A confession? Hysterics?
Nance (*gaily, with a touch of melodrama*) Maybe they expected to find the verdict in your eyes!
Lizzie (*laughing*) Most of 'em had reached the verdict—in their hearts—before entering the courthouse. The trial, for them, was to be a mere formality.
Henry Furthermore, witnesses will be introduced offering evidence of a young woman attempting to buy poison. I think, gentlemen, you will be satisfied that there can be no question that the person who made this application for this deadly poison was none other but the prisoner.
Lizzie William H. Moody. That was his name—the prosecutor . . .
Emma Persecutor, more likely!
Annie (*excitedly*) Did he really believe you guilty?

Lizzie (*wrily*) I never got around to asking him!

Henry Evidence will be presented in this courtroom, corroborating that the prisoner did not, in fact, visit the loft in the barn, as she has stated, but that she was, in truth, in the house all the time. (*He paces for a moment, then turns sharply to the jury*) Does that sound like the actions of an innocent woman? (*Dramatic pause*) Would an innocent woman lie? (*Pause*) Because lie she did. Not once, but several times. (*Pause*) On the question of the dress, for instance. She handed into custody a dress which she claims to have been wearing on the morning these atrocious crimes were committed. (*Pause*) We shall produce a witness who saw Lizzie Borden burning a dress a short while after the murders. At a time when the prisoner knew the Sheriff's office to be searching for blood-stained clothing, she elected to burn a dress! (*Pause. With a slight smile*) She says it was stained with—paint!

Emma (*impulsively*) She'd been talking of burning it for months!

Henry I suggest, gentlemen, that this was the dress she'd been wearing on the morning of the crimes, and that she was sending up in smoke the evidence of her guilt.

Lizzie (*calmly*) An eloquent man, Mr Moody . . .

Annie moves into the light, bringing a chair with her. She sits on it

Henry I further suggest that the stains were not that of paint! (*He turns to Annie*) You are Mrs Adelaide Churchill?

Annie (*nodding*) Adelaide P. Churchill.

Henry (*with a slight smile*) I stand corrected.

Annie You're welcome, I'm sure.

Henry (*slowly*) Now, I want you to think back to that terrible morning when Lizzie Borden asked you to go into her house for . . .

Annie Will I ever forget it? For so long as I live it will be imprinted—in indelible letters of fire—on my brain! Oh, I swear to you I will never . . .

Emma (*shortly*) Addie wasn't a bit like that. (*Pause*) She was a normal human being.

Annie (*directly to Emma*) If you think you can do better, then you can come and do it. I'm sick to death of jumping in and out of character, like a Jack-in-the-box.

Lizzie Pay no heed, Annie.

Annie Besides, if what I hear of her is true, the real Mrs Churchill would fade away under these bright lights. She sounds as dull as ditchwater!

Nance Come along, dear heart. Back into character with you.

Slight pause

Annie I'll need my cue again.

Tom You mean we've got to suffer that speech about letters of fire all over again.

Annie (*condescendingly*) All right, Henry. We'll miss the big speech. Just start from where you want, and I'll *ad lib* until such time as I can pick up my cue.

Nance (*ironically*) Spoken like a real old trouper!

Henry ponders on Annie's idea, and slips into character again

Henry What I really want to know, Mrs Churchill, is this—do you remember the dress the prisoner was wearing that morning?
Annie Let me see . . . Yes, I do remember.
Henry Then will you kindly describe it, for the benefit of the jury?
Annie Well—it looked like a light-blue-and-white groundwork—with—a dark navy-blue diamond on it.
Henry Are you sure of that?
Annie (*indignantly*) I most certainly am!
Henry A light-blue-and-white groundwork—with a dark navy-blue diamond?
Annie That is so.
Henry I have here a silk dress that was handed into custody by the prisoner . . . (*He shows her an imaginary dress*)
Lizzie (*sotto voce*) Note his cunning use of the word "silk"!
Henry Is this the one she was wearing that morning?
Annie (*vehemently*) No sir!
Henry You are definite on that point?
Annie Most definite. No-one wears a silk dress in the morning, for doing the household chores. (*She buries her face in her hands, then looks up, sadly*) I'm sorry, Lizzie. I didn't mean to—to . . . But it's the truth, isn't it? (*She stares forlornly into her lap*)
Emma It wasn't silk. Merely Bengalese silk, which . . .
Lizzie Which is a somewhat pretentious title for a mixture of cotton and silk—with rather more emphasis on the cotton than on the silk.

Annie seems a little unsure as to what to do next

Henry Is something wrong, Annie?
Annie Is it worth getting up? I've only got to come and sit down again as— as . . . (*She appeals to Nance*) Who am I next?
Nance Alice Russell.
Annie (*to Henry*) As Alice Russell. So can't I just stay?

Henry fusses furiously with the tails of his coat

Henry I guess so!
Annie All right, Henry. Go ahead. I'm Alice Russell.
Nance Congratulations! We thought you'd never make it.

With ill-concealed impatience Henry takes a few paces, to regain his character

Henry Miss Russell, you have already testified that you saw the prisoner burning a dress on the Sunday morning, three days after the homicide?
Annie Yes, sir.
Henry Will you please give us a description of the dress?
Annie It was a cheap cotton Bedford cord.
Henry What was its colour?
Annie Light-blue ground, with a dark figure. A small figure.
Henry A diamond, perhaps?

Annie Well, I . . .
Tom (*from the darkness*) Objection! The witness is being led.
Henry Thank you, Miss Russell (*He smiles at Tom*) Your witness, Mr Robinson.

Henry goes from the light and Tom moves into it

Tom Regarding the dress the prisoner burned—can you give me any further description of the small dark figure?
Annie No, sir. Only that it was small.
Tom Then it could have been a diamond—or a flower—or a spot—or . . .
Henry (*from the darkness*) Objection! Counsel is leading the witness!

Tom satirically bows to him, and turns again to Annie

Tom Can you remember the dress worn by the defendant on the morning of the crime?
Annie No, sir.
Tom Nothing at all about it?
Annie No, sir.

Tom paces for a moment

Tom To return to the one which was burned. You testified that you had seen it on two occasions only—this is correct?
Annie Yes, sir.
Tom Will you repeat those occasions?
Annie The first time was in the early spring.
Tom Was your attention called to it in any way?
Annie Well, I went along one evening, and she had it on. She asked me if I liked it, because it was new, and I told her I thought it very pretty— or something like that—and I didn't see it again until—this time.
Tom The time it was burned?
Annie Yes, sir.
Tom To make it perfectly clear—from the time you saw it on Miss Lizzie Borden in the spring, you did not see it again until the Sunday morning after the homicide?
Annie No, sir.
Tom Thank you, Miss Russell. That will be all.

Annie moves out of the light. Tom stays there

Emma (*triumphantly*) You see! She'd have recognized it if Lizzie'd been wearing it on the morning they were talking about!
Nance What puzzles me, Lizzie, is why the police didn't find the dress— if it was bloodstained—when they searched the house. After all, it wasn't burned until three days after. In full view of Alice Russell, Emma, and any policemen or passing sightseers who cared to be staring through the open windows of the kitchen.
Emma They tried to pretend they hadn't searched properly.
Lizzie Despite having searched the house, the barn, and the garden on the day of the slayings—and the following day—and the day after that.

Emma For the second of the searches they even brought Medical Examiner Dolan—an expert on detecting bloodstains on clothing—but he found nothing.

Lizzie They had Assistant Marshal Fleet on the stand—

Henry moves into the light and sits down

—but Mr Robinson's cross-questioning soon showed that they had really searched, but found nothing.

Tom enters the lighted area

Tom (*to Henry*) . . . and you were searching for clothing with blood on it?

Henry Well, we did not search quite as thoroughly as we might have . . .

Tom You took each dress and looked at it? Is that so?

Henry Yes, sir. I think it is about so.

Tom Were you looking to see if you could find any bloodstained garment?

Henry Not very closely, it was . . .

Tom But that is what you had in mind?

Henry Yes, sir.

Slight pause

Tom Was there any blood on the dresses of the maid, Bridget Sullivan? Known in the Borden household as "Maggie"?

Henry On her clothes?

Tom That is what I asked you.

Henry No. I didn't discover anything in the line of blood.

Tom You didn't really look for blood on Bridget's dresses, did you?

Henry (*evasively*) I looked at Bridget's dresses . . .

Tom Will you please tell the jury how you looked?

Henry We looked at the dresses as they were—some were thrown on the bed.

Tom Were there any in the closet?

Henry There were some in a closet.

Tom Did you take them down?

Henry I threw them on the bed, that was all.

Slight pause

Tom You searched Miss Lizzie Borden's room?

Henry Yes, sir.

Tom Did you examine her dresses carefully—more carefully, say, than you examined those of Bridget?

Henry I don't know, sir. I think so.

Tom These dresses—they were in a closet?

Henry Some of them were, I think.

Tom Did you take them out to look at them?

Henry No, sir. Not to take them down, but just looked at them.

Tom "Not to take them down"? But you and two officers were there making a search, weren't you?

Henry Yes, sir.

Tom Some, you said, were in a closet. Where were the rest?
Henry On the bed.
Tom Did you look at them?
Henry Very briefly . . .
Tom They would have had many spots on them if they'd been worn by the murderer. Did you examine each of them—"briefly"?
Henry I think so.
Tom There were three of you. If you weren't examining the dresses, what were the three of you doing in the room?
Henry (*miserably*) I guess we did look at each of them . . .
Tom But found no stains?
Henry No, sir.
Tom Did you search any other closets in Miss Borden's room?
Henry (*pause*) Yes, sir.
Tom Trunks?
Henry Yes, sir.
Tom Drawers?
Henry Yes, sir.
Tom Did you take out the things to examine them?
Henry Yes, sir.

Slight pause

Tom So, if there had been a bloodstained dress in Lizzie's room, you would have been sure to find it?
Henry I guess so.
Tom I'm not asking for "guesses", Mr Fleet, but facts! Is that so, or not? If there'd been a bloodstained dress you would have been sure to see it?
Henry Yes, sir.
Tom Thank you. (*A slight pause, as he changes direction*) Now may we turn to the handle-less hatchet—the alleged murder weapon—which was found in the cellar? (*He shows him an imaginary hatchet*) You recognize it?
Henry Yes, sir.
Tom I've no doubt that you'll confirm that when it was discovered it was covered in ashes?
Henry Yes, sir.
Tom (*to the "jury"*) I stress the fact of the ashes, gentlemen, since, as you have heard, it is the contention of the prosecution that this hatchet was used to commit the crimes and afterwards washed and thrust into ashes, whilst wet, thus accounting for its condition. (*To Henry*) Will you please repeat where this was found?
Henry On a shelf. In the cellar of the house.
Tom Where—if my information is correct—stands a coal furnace?
Henry Yes, sir.
Tom So—naturally—in this celler there is much ash?
Henry Well, I . . .
Tom (*sharply*) Is there, or is there not?
Henry There is.

Tom In fact, there is a huge pile a few feet only from the shelf on which the alleged murder weapon was discovered?
Henry Yes, sir.
Tom How large a pile, in your estimation?
Henry Oh, that I couldn't say . . .
Tom Roughly. (*Slight pause*) Five bucketful—or ten—or a hundred?
Henry About fifty, I should think.
Tom In other words, a considerable deal of ash?
Henry Yes, sir.
Tom Yet, in your estimation, this weapon could not have become covered in ash naturally, but must have been first plunged into water, and then deliberately coated with it?
Henry Well, I . . .
Tom Thank you. That's all for the moment.

Henry moves out of the light

And now for the testimony of Doctor Wood.

Henry moves back into the light and sits down again

Henry (*with a tiny wave to those outside the light*) It's me again, folks!
Tom Have you had time to assume the character of Doctor Wood?
Henry I think so.
Nance (*drily*) "Think so"? Such indecision belongs to your previous scintillating cameo.

Henry decides to ignore her. A slight pause

Tom Doctor Wood, I am informed you have tested this hatchet for bloodstains?
Henry That is correct.
Tom Did you find traces of any?
Henry No.
Tom They could have been removed?
Henry (*doubtfully*) Bloodstains could be removed, but not by a quick washing. (*He takes the hatchet and points to it*) You see, on this hatchet, for instance, blood would cling in these angles here. It would have to be done by cold water, and very thoroughly washed in order to remove it. Also, this slot on the inner edge furnishes a good refuge for any blood to gather. It would be quite a place to clean, assuming that any blood got on it. (*He hands it back to Tom*) Anyhow, that hatchet hasn't been washed in years.
Tom How can you be sure of that?
Henry See for yourself. There is white dirt in there. It's ground in, showing it to have been there for a long time.
Tom In other words, Doctor, the hatchet has not been washed, nor does it bear bloodstains?
Henry Quite.
Emma (*in a loud whisper*) You see! They even had the wrong murder weapon in the courthouse!

Tom I'd like now to move to the question of poison. You examined, I believe, the stomachs of the deceased?

Henry (*nodding*) Both Mr and Mrs Borden.

Tom It has been suggested that poison was administered to them the day before the crimes at issue here . . .

Henry I found no evidence of any kind.

Tom Of any kind whatever?

Henry (*shaking his head*) In neither case.

Tom (*smiling*) Thank you, Doctor. That is all.

Henry gets up and moves out of the light. Tom follows him. The main Lights go up

Annie But what about the man who identified you as having attempted to purchase the prussic acid?

Emma Sensation seeker! Eli Bence was a fool! Besides, she'd a' needed to a' been mad to even think of using prussic acid.

Annie Why?

Emma Well, naturally, since it figured so prominently at the trial, I read up on it, and, do you know, it's hardly ever used in murder cases?

Annie Doesn't it work?

Emma Huh! It works too fast—that's the trouble. Less than a minute. Folk would a' been mighty suspicious if we'd all a' dropped dead.

Annie laughs

It's no laughing matter, miss. (*Pause*) Then there's its—very distinctive odour—it's easily detected . . .

Annie But, Eli Bence . . .?

Lizzie When cross-examined, he stated he had identified me by my voice, in the dark. It was "thin and tremulous", he said.

Emma There was another to identify her. A student named Jennings, who'd been sitting in the drug-store when she supposedly went in to ask for the poison.

Lizzie He, too, recognized me by my voice. Because it was loud and harsh.

Emma So much for the poison nonsense.

Lizzie But the really important evidence was that which established I was in the barn, like I said.

The main Lights dim, leaving a circle of light. Tom moves into it

It came from an ice-cream vendor, named Lubinsky . . .

Henry enters the spot, and sits down. He accentuates the awkwardness of the accent, making it hard to understand

Tom Your name is Hyman Lubinsky?

Henry That is right. I am emigrated from Russia.

Tom What is your occupation, Mr Lubinsky?

Henry (*puzzled*) Eh?

Tom You sell ice-cream?

Henry (*nodding*) For a store on Main Street. With a horse and wagon, I sell it.

Tom Will you please tell us, in your own words, what you did on the morning of August fourth?

Henry Well, when I awakened, I go to Second Street, which is where the horse and wagon is kept in the stable, and then I rode it past the house where the Misses Bordens lives.

Tom At what time was that?

Henry Just after eleven o'clock.

Tom Are you sure of the time?

Henry But of course! Because of the hour so late. I am sleeping for too long, and also I am having to wait for the horse, while she is fed.

Tom So you passed the house a little after eleven?

Henry Is that not what I am saying?

Tom What did you see?

Henry I see a lady come out of the way from the barn, right to the house.

Tom From the barn?

Henry Is my English not so good?

Tom I merely wish to establish the point.

Henry (*puzzled*) Eh?

Tom You saw a lady come out of the barn, and go into the house?

Henry That is so.

Tom Perhaps this lady was the maid, Bridget Sullivan?

Henry No, it was not she. Because the maid I have seen.

Tom You know her?

Henry To her I have delivered the ice-cream, and seen her, I am telling you.

The spot fades, the main Lights come up

Emma The owner of the stable, and also a travelling salesman established the time Lubinsky passed the house, and saw Lizzie.

Annie But I thought the police had evidence she had not been in the barn?

Emma Not evidence. The word of a no-good patrolman.

Lizzie William H. Medley.

Emma Huh! Meddler, more likely!

Tom The one who said there were no footprints in the loft?

Annie How did they prove otherwise?

Lizzie First of all, two boys gave evidence they'd crept up there, to look out of the window. To see what was going on in the yard. That would have been before Medley arrived on the scene. Then there was a local newspaper reporter who went into the barn, and testified in court that there had been several people up in the loft before Medley arrived.

Emma "Long before he arrived!" That was the newspaperman's own words. "Long before!"

Henry From what you've told us, Lizzie, it seems a miracle—to say the least—that you were ever committed to trial.

Nance (*slyly*) Have you forgotten what you said earlier, Henry? You're hearing Lizzie's side of the story. The story of the defence.

Emma (*stifling a yawn*) And why not? Why shouldn't you? After all, she was innocent. After thirteen days of careful consideration the jury found her Not Guilty. That was the verdict! So why shouldn't she sound innocent?

Annie What a relief it must a' been to get it over with. I should think . . .

Emma Huh! You think that was the end of it? You think folk was prepared to believe the jury?

Lizzie The newspapers still wanted stories. They waited outside the house . . .

Emma One reporter even stole into the house. But Lizzie said nothing to any of 'em!

Lizzie So they speculated—and exaggerated . . .

Emma One of the newspapers ran a story of how Lizzie asked our next-door neighbour to remove the fence between our properties, and how he'd replied that if Lizzie Borden was to be his neighbour, then he'd build it higher.

Lizzie A foolish story, really. Why should I want the fence removed? I got little enough privacy, anyhow.

Emma I told you at the time you should a' sued 'em for printing such trash.

Lizzie That would have been to no purpose but to give them the opportunity to bring up the trial all over again.

Emma They also went on suggesting that maybe the murderer—or murderess—may still be in the town. Everyone knew who they meant.

Nance Was there any particular reason for moving to this house?

Lizzie We always preferred this part of the town.

Annie Why didn't you leave Fall River, and start all over again?

Lizzie (*laughing ruefully*) There was nothing to run away from. (*Pause*) Nor to. Besides, there have been Bordens here for nigh on two hundred and seventy years—so it's kind a' like home for me.

The church clock strikes midnight. Emma stifles a further yawn, which Nance notices

Nance Is it midnight so soon?

Tom Time for broomsticks and long-legged beasties.

Nance You wouldn't be talking of the landlady, by any chance?

Tom You make a neat little figure on a broomstick, yourself.

Nance Flatterer! (*To Lizzie*) I hope we haven't outstayed our welcome. I think it's time we let you and Emma go to bed.

Lizzie It's been wonderful having you here. We seldom get visitors.

Tom What Nance is really worried about is losing her beauty sleep. As though it matters, at her age.

Lizzie (*smiling*) Have some more coffee before you go?

Nance No, thank you.

Lizzie I guess it'll be a long time before we see any more theatre-folk in this house. If ever.

Annie (*impulsively*) Should I happen around these parts again, I'll drop in on you, Lizzie!

Lizzie You mean that?

Annie You bet I do. I'll never forget meeting you. Never! It's been most

exciting. One of the most exciting things in my whole life. Just imagine!
Meeting a real . . . (*She stops and becomes a little flustered*)
Nance (*not very helpfully*) "Character", dear heart?

Lizzie smiles

Lizzie (*to put Annie at ease*) It's been equally exciting for me to meet all of
you. Yours is such a romantic life—where you can wipe away tragedy
with a pot of cream and a rag. Where the lights are warm and coloured—
to make you look beautiful—as you move around in gorgeous
costumes . . .
Henry You're not envious, are you?
Lizzie (*after a pause, laughing*) I'm not that adventurous. I wish I were.
Emma Nonsense, Lizzie! Going to Europe was adventurous.
Lizzie No it wasn't, Emma. It was simply a journey I made with a lot of
highly respectable ladies.
Annie I'd love to go to Europe!
Nance For the moment, dear heart, let us content ourselves with going
back to our lodging-house.
Lizzie With whom are you staying?
Nance Mrs Thompson, down by the theatre.
Emma (*disapprovingly*) Isn't she something of a blue-stocking?
Nance That's no blue stocking, honey, but varicose veins! Do you know,
she has found no less than one million ways of telling us how she
doesn't consider theatre-folk monsters, like everyone else. She tells us,
and tells us, and tells us . . . But I notice how we eat off matching plates
with the dog, whilst she uses bone china for herself.
Lizzie Oh dear. Is it so terrible there?
Tom Nance has an infallible knack for being able to turn any place into
hell. It's an affliction I think she was born with.
Nance Are you going to deny she rattles about the house with the largest
bunch of keys in the world, locking up everything from us?
Lizzie You must find small-town prejudice very annoying.
Nance What makes you think it happens only in small towns? (*She surveys
herself in a mirror*) God! You're beautiful, Nance! Well, I guess I'm
ready to face whoever's abroad in the streets at this hour.
Henry All that remains is for Nance to make her big exit.
Lizzie (*rising*) We'll see you to the door. Won't we, Emma?
Emma (*reluctantly*) If you say so, Lizzie.
Lizzie (*laughing*) She's afraid the neighbours'll see her talking to you
immoral theatre-folk.
Emma Lizzie!

*As Emma gets to her feet, yawning, Tom, Annie and Henry move towards the
door*

Henry Are you sure we can't persuade you to tell us who you think was
the real killer?
Lizzie No, Henry. But I'm flattered to hear that you now think it might
have been someone else.

Emma (*shortly*) What else should he think?

*Henry goes. Annie and Tom follow. Emma follows. Nance makes her exit,
arm in arm with Lizzie*

Nance (*as they go*) I'll write you, Lizzie. We must keep in touch.
Lizzie Perhaps we'll meet again before you move on?
Nance Leave a message with Mrs Thompson. Don't bother to seal it, since
I've no doubt she'll steam it open. Wouldn't be surprised if she kept a
kettle on the boil all the time, waiting for us to receive mail. Rattling a
triumphant march on her goddam keys! Do you know, there's only one
room in the house she doesn't lock . . .?

*The room is now empty. A murmur of voices is heard as Lizzie and Emma bid
their guests good night. A tinkling of glass is heard*

*A moment later the curtains covering the french windows are stealthily
parted and Bridget Sullivan enters. She is a large-boned, ruddy-complex-
ioned woman of thirty-nine, tidily—but not smartly—dressed. She is
slightly unsteady on her feet, being a little drunk!*

*After flicking through the pages of the scrapbook, and a fleeting reconnoitre
of the room, scanning any papers lying about, Bridget moves to the table,
tries the punch by plunging her fingers into it and licking them, then pours
herself some, with her back to the door*

Lizzie and Emma enter

*Emma stifles a scream. Bridget turns suddenly. Lizzie advances a few paces
towards her*

Lizzie (*sharply*) How did you get in?
Bridget Wouldn't you be after recognizing me?
Lizzie Bridget Sullivan. So it was you who followed me?
Bridget It was something of a surprise, not finding you in Second Street,
and I was beginning to think I'd be robbed of the pleasure of seeing the
two of youse, but then, with the luck of the Irish, as they say, I sees you
outside the theatre, and here I am.

*During the above, Emma moves to the french windows, and sees the shattered
glass*

Emma You've broken the window. (*To Lizzie*) I'll go for the police. (*She
moves toward the hall, to get a coat, but Lizzie stops her with a gesture*)
Lizzie No!
Emma But she . . .
Lizzie No. (*Pause*) Later, maybe.

Bridget sits, and surveys them with a mocking smile

Bridget Sure it's a fine thing to find the pair of youse unchanged by your
bitter experience.
Lizzie You've changed. Since when was it the fashion for serving-maids
to be so brazen?

Bridget You'll not rile me, Lizzie Borden. You see, I'm not a skivvy any longer. (*Giggling*) That way I'd be an old maid. (*Mockingly*) I see neither of yourselves has taken a man to be your lawfully-wedded husband?

Emma Lizzie's had the chance, but . . .

Lizzie Hush, Emma. It's no concern of Bridget Sullivan.

Emma (*to Bridget—defiantly*) A clergyman, no less!

Bridget Sure, a fine mating that would have been. Did he find out the terrible truth?

She directs this at Emma, whose face and silence confirm it to be true

Ah, but men of the cloth have their reputations to think of, you understand.

Lizzie (*ignoring this*) Why did you break in, like a common thief? Have folk stopped opening their doors to you?

Bridget Well, I'm the soul of tact, and I wouldn't want to be after interrupting anything, so I thought I'd just take a peek to see if you was otherwise engaged. And I saw you was, so thought I'd wait until they left. It surprised me . . .

Emma But the men looked outside!

Bridget A fine pair they was, too. Blind as bats. I was in the bushes, not more than five feet away from them. It surprised me, I can tell you, to see you entertaining the like. Such painted women . . .! Could hardly believe me eyes.

Lizzie From the quantity of liquor you appear to have consumed, I'm mightily surprised you can see anything at all.

Bridget Oh, we're hardened drinkers—me husband and me.

She watches for the effect of this revelation. Lizzie shows no reaction, but Emma does

Emma Then your name's not Bridget Sullivan any longer?

Bridget I married a man named Sullivan. I couldn't bear to be parting with the name.

Lizzie An Irishman?

Bridget To be sure. You don't think I'd be after marrying below me station, do you now? (*She laughs, and drains her cup*)

Lizzie Where did you meet him?

Bridget In a tiny place they call Anaconda. We live there. He's a traveller, and when he told me he'd be coming to Fall River, I thought I'd be after having a marvellous opportunity for lookin' to see how youse was doing. So here I am, and I must say youse don't look very pleased to see me.

Emma We're not.

Lizzie Where is he, at this moment?

Bridget Talking business, with a client.

Lizzie (*after a pause*) On what did you spend the money I gave you to return to Ireland just after the trial?

Emma (*sharply*) What money?

Bridget (*smiling*) Did you not tell your own sister of the little present?

Lizzie No.

Bridget Why not, pray?
Lizzie I had my reasons. Your glass is empty.
Bridget Would you be invitin' me to have another?
Lizzie (*shrugging her shoulders*) It'll only be thrown away if you don't drink it.

Bridget goes to the table and helps herself to punch. She remains there, watching the sisters, and enjoying the scene

Emma I'm shocked, Lizzie. Shocked!
Lizzie Why should you be shocked?
Emma There were rumours you'd given her money—and I denied them.
Lizzie It was a foolish thing for me to do. I didn't think.
Emma People said you'd bribed her. Given her money, and sent her away because she knew too much.
Lizzie (*resignedly*) I know.
Emma (*frightened*) It's not true, is it?
Lizzie Bridget's there. Ask her!
Emma Why didn't you tell me? We've no secrets from each other. Why lie to me about this?
Lizzie (*sharply*) I've never lied, Emma. (*Pause*) You've never asked me, directly, if it was true I'd given her money . . .
Emma You've not been fair. I've believed in your innocence, and stood by you all these years, with mud clinging to me . . .
Lizzie (*cuttingly*) Thank you for your devotion, dear sister. If a small thing like this shatters the foundation of your faith in me, I suggest you look to the back of your mind to see what monstrous accusations lie there! And whether you've ever really trusted in my innocence! (*Angrily*) There's Bridget Sullivan, standing before you. Why not ask her? Are you so afraid she'll confirm what you've always really believed all these years? When I gave her the money I told her the reason. Go on! Ask her why.

Emma is shattered by this outburst, and sits looking extremely miserable. Slowly, she looks up at Bridget, but cannot bring herself to ask

Bridget Would you like to know what she told me?

She waits for a reply, but Emma remains silent

She said, "Here's the money for you to return home to Ireland, where, I'll be thinking, you'll soon forget all about what you have seen and experienced these past weeks." At least, that's how I best remember it.
Emma (*to Bridget*) "Forget what you'd seen"? What had you seen?

A slight pause

Bridget You heard my evidence.
Emma (*to Lizzie*) What did you mean . . .?
Lizzie She'd seen the bodies, and the trial . . .
Emma (*suspiciously*) Is that all you meant?
Lizzie (*impatiently*) Oh, believe what you want!

Bridget (*in a slightly mocking tone*) Now don't let me come between youse
good ladies.
Emma I don't understand why you didn't tell me.
Lizzie At first, I had intended to. But, once the rumours began, I considered
it better for no-one to know. Not even you, Emma. That's why the
newspapers had nothing further to write scurrilous, sensational columns
on. They'd have seen an admission of guilt in it.
Bridget (*slyly*) Your sister is right, Emma. I think it would have sounded
a wee bit suspicious. I remember thinking, myself, when it happened,
how odd it was, her giving me my passage money, and a little else,
beside.
Lizzie (*drily*) You had sufficient prudence, I notice, not to mention it at
the time.
Bridget I was never the one for looking a gift-horse in the mouth. (*She
helps herself to some more punch*) Wouldn't I be the fool to? Me, with
never more than two pairs of stockings to me name. And them darned
until there was hardly a patch of stocking left. But youse fine ladies
would never understand that. Why should you? Youse was born in the
lap of luxury. "Besides," I told myself, "she'll never miss what she's
after giving me. It's no more than a drop in the ocean for her." (*She
gulps at her punch*) But I wasted it, going back to the old country.
Everything, everywhere, was as bad as the day I'd left it.
Lizzie Then why did you go?
Bridget I didn't know when I went, did I? I'd thought a lot about me
family. And I was fool enough to think everything would have changed,
and that there'd be enough food and work for us to stay together.
(*Bitterly*) It was like expecting the little people to come out and work
their magic. (*Further gulps at her punch*) So I stayed there for a few years,
and I saved me pennies till I was able to come back.

*Emma remains deep in thought during most of this speech. She speaks
suddenly*

Emma If you've come back to blackmail Lizzie, you've wasted your time.
We'll see you in the county gaol first.
Bridget (*laughing*) What an evil mind you have.
Emma Besides, Lizzie knows the identity of the real killer.

Pause

Bridget Does she, now?
Emma Tell her, Lizzie.
Lizzie A moment ago we were debating whether or not I was the real
killer.
Emma (*contritely*) I'm sorry.

Bridget refills her cup

Bridget If you know who was the one responsible, I'm surprised you said
nothing at the time you were under arrest.
Lizzie I didn't know at the time of my arrest.

Bridget Is that so? And when were you after making this discovery?
Lizzie A while after my acquittal. The facts kept haunting me. For instance, I couldn't forget how the killer had entered the house and slain my stepmother whilst I was in one of the other rooms.
Bridget I fail to see how he could have entered without me seein' him.
Lizzie Yes, I thought on that, too. You were cleaning the outside windows, so it certainly would have been difficult for him to get in. (*Pause*) Also, he'd have to get out again, and walk along the main street unnoticed, which would hardly be likely, with his clothes drenched in blood.
Bridget Just what are you suggesting?
Lizzie (*cunningly*) Well, you see, it had occurred to me that if your testimony was slightly inaccurate—after all, everyone was confused at the time—I think I know how he may have got in.

Bridget gulps her drink, and thinks on this

Bridget What do you mean?
Lizzie For instance, the doctor says she died between nine a.m. and ten . . .
Bridget I saw her alive at nine-thirty, as I went out to clean the windows.
Lizzie You then stated that you stayed outside, cleaning the windows, for one hour, until ten-thirty, and it was during that time, whilst you were outside the house, that she was killed.
Bridget Sure it was.
Lizzie Supposing you'd made a mistake, and actually finished cleaning 'em at—say—a little before ten? That way, someone could a' crept in while you were doing the inside windows, and you wouldn't a' noticed him.
Bridget (*shaking her head*) No. I finished cleaning the outside windows at ten-thirty. Of that I am certain. And there was only yourself and Mrs Borden in the house. I'd like to help you with this—theory you have—by proving that someone could have got in, but I was definitely outside from nine-thirty until ten-thirty.
Lizzie (*slyly*) Oh, but you have helped me a little already.
Bridget (*suspiciously*) In what way, may I ask?
Lizzie Simply by being adamant on a point to which I have given a great deal of thought. You see, when I went into the kitchen that morning you were just finishing off washing the dishes, prior to going out and doing the windows. It was nine a.m. I figure you must have started the outside windows at about five after nine.
Bridget Then why wouldn't you be mentioning it at the time?
Lizzie (*shrugging*) It didn't seem that important. An error of twenty-five minutes. Everyone was a little confused. However, if you were capable of a twenty-five minute error in one direction, why not half an hour the other way? Did it really take one-and-a-half hours to clean seven windows?
Bridget One hour. From nine-thirty to ten-thirty. And I talked a little, over the fence, with the servant next door.
Lizzie We know that. For just a few minutes.
Bridget And I was sick outside.

Lizzie We know that, also.
Bridget For fifteen minutes. Jesus! I thought I'd die!
Lizzie What made you sick for a whole fifteen minutes, Bridget?
Bridget The food. You know it was. Youse was all sick.
Lizzie It was the bread made us sick. The bread that you went out and bought. But you didn't want any. What made you sick, Bridget?
Bridget They didn't prove it was the bread.
Lizzie That may be so, but we were all sick after eating it, nevertheless. What made you sick?
Bridget What's the use of me answering, when you refuses to believe me?
Lizzie All I want to know is, why it took you so long to clean seven windows?
Bridget I wanted them done properly.
Lizzie Didn't you always do them properly?
Bridget They'd not been done for some time.
Lizzie They were supposed to be done regularly.
Bridget That's what she said.
Lizzie Who?
Bridget Mrs Borden.
Lizzie When?
Bridget A couple a' days before. "Isn't it time you did those windows, Maggie?" she said. "Me name's Bridget", I told her. But youse was all the same. I could tell you me name's Bridget till I was blue in the face, but you never tried to remember.
Emma We called all our maids Maggie.
Bridget I'm sure they must have found it flatterin'!
Emma The first maid we could remember was called Maggie.
Lizzie Did Mrs Borden mention the windows again?
Bridget Every time she saw me.
Lizzie Then why weren't they done?
Bridget I'd only one pair of hands to keep the four of youse happy.
Lizzie Did she mention them on the morning she died?
Bridget You know she did.
Lizzie I know only what you told me. At nine-thirty, wasn't it?
Bridget Yes.
Lizzie At no other time?
Bridget As soon as she told me, I went out and did 'em.
Lizzie Uncle John Vinnicum said she mentioned the windows a little after seven a.m.
Bridget Then he was mistaken.
Lizzie It would appear everyone got their facts wrong, except you.
Bridget I had nothing to lie about. I was innocent.
Lizzie We're all innocent, until proven guilty.
Bridget If you're after thinking you can prove I did it, then you're wasting your time.
Lizzie But you must admit you had the opportunity?

Bridget pours herself some more punch as she deliberates

Bridget If you're putting it in that fashion, I suppose I had. But why should I do it? Answer me that?

Lizzie (*thoughtfully*) I must confess, you have me there.

Bridget (*more relaxed*) Sure, we had occasional hard words, but . . .

Lizzie Hard words?

Bridget Like about the windows. "I want to see them done, and no more dallying," she said. "I've only one pair of hands," I told her. Things like that. Nothing serious.

Lizzie You often answered her in that manner?

Bridget Not when there was others present. They wouldn't have understood.

Lizzie Understood what?

Bridget Why, how even a servant has feelings, and can be angry. Youse two wouldn't understand. We're just arms and legs for supplying your creature comforts, so far as youse are concerned.

Lizzie But she understood?

Bridget Sometimes she did, sometimes she didn't.

Lizzie What happened on the occasions when she didn't understand?

Bridget She'd firmly put me in my place.

Lizzie Didn't you resent that?

Bridget She made me feel like dirt!

Lizzie Did you hate her for it?

Bridget sips her drink, and answers carefully

Bridget I got so I could stop listening when I chose to.

Lizzie And did you "choose to" on the morning she told you to get out and clean the windows?

Bridget I said nothing. I just went.

Lizzie So, the last time you saw her alive, you weren't exactly friendly?

Bridget I didn't say that.

Lizzie (*thoughtfully*) Another thing that has often occurred to me is that your alibi placed you outside the house at the time of the crime . . .

Bridget Oh, so it's an alibi, is it? If you're after thinking . . .

Lizzie (*relentlessly*) But you, yourself, set the time of the crime!

Emma (*puzzled*) What are you saying, Lizzie?

Bridget She's trying to . . .

Lizzie The doctor said she died between nine and ten. Who established she was alive at nine-thirty? Bridget. And who placed herself safely outside the house for the next hour? Bridget! (*Directly to Bridget*) Furthermore, it is a fact that you left the house at five after nine, and not nine-thirty.

Bridget You must be mad.

Lizzie Let me tell you what could have happened . . .

Bridget You're trying . . .

Lizzie No! Just listen to my—theory, as you call it. It's not an accusation.

Bridget I should hope not. If it's accusations you'll be makin' I'll soon have ye payin' for 'em in a court of law!

Lizzie We'll see how you feel after you've heard me. (*In a slightly softer tone*) Finish off the punch, Bridget. It'd be a pity to waste it.

Bridget helps herself to more punch

Bridget (*aggressively*) Well? I'm waitin' to hear this fine theory.

Lizzie Let's assume—like I said—that you went out at five after nine, and began cleaning the windows. Then, at about twenty after nine you saw Mr Borden leave, and . . .

Bridget But I didn't . . .

Lizzie So you testified at the trial. However, let us say that you did see him leave. That left only Mrs Borden and myself in the house—she, upstairs, at the front of the house, and me, downstairs, in the dining-room at the side of the house. Now, you could easily have come back inside, seen me busy ironing, gone upstairs, where she was dusting the room, killed her, and—

Bridget If this is what . . .

Lizzie —killed her, changed your clothing, and been outside the house again a little after nine-thirty. And, had anyone seen you going out at that time, fine, you were perfectly safe, since you, yourself, had given the evidence that she was still alive at nine-thirty.

Bridget laughs, but not convincingly

Bridget If this is what happens to old women who live on their own, then I'm glad I'm not one of youse. Jesus! You're as mad as a March hare!

Lizzie Also, you were alone in the house with father when he died.

Bridget If I took you to court for this, they'd certify you, for sure!

Lizzie (*unmoved*) Then there's the question of the bloodstained clothing. I was not allowed out of the house, so how could I possibly dispose of it? Or the axe, for that matter?

Bridget You burned the dress. I wonder at the mentality of the men on that jury for not realizin' the evidence they had before them.

Lizzie (*as though Bridget had not spoken*) You left the house, though, Bridget. Each night you left, to stay with a cousin. And you carried a bundle of clothing.

Bridget Me—nightdress. Heavens, I'd be needin' that, wouldn't I?

Lizzie Why couldn't you bear to sleep in the house?

Bridget With a madman prowling the town?

Lizzie You'd have been safer with us. The place was surrounded by policemen.

Emma Alice Russell stayed. She wasn't afraid.

Lizzie What were you frightened of, Bridget? Ghosts? Was it fear that you'd see the eyes of Mrs Borden looking up at you as you struck that first blow on her forehead? What was the expression that haunted you? Surprise? Terror?

Bridget No! No! Listen to me, and I'll . . .

Lizzie Is that what made you sick in the yard for fifteen minutes? Eh, Bridget?

Bridget (*appealing to Emma*) You listen to me, and I'll tell you what kind of a creature you've lived with all these years!

Emma I don't want to . . .

Bridget You got my sympathy when they talk of your devotion. I'll say ye have. Just wait until you hear the kind of monster you've been wastin' it on! (*She begins pacing the room*) She's quite right. I did venture back into the house. I was feelin' a tiny bit faint, so I went in for a minute, to rest, and get myself a drink o' water. Little did I realize what I was to be seeing. (*She pauses, to calculate the effect she is having*) Anyhow, I went in—went in—and I heard this noise—like—like—I can't explain what it sounded like. It was coming from upstairs, so I crept up, to see what was going on. When I got to the top o' the stairs—you can imagine my surprise at seein' a pair of shoes outside the room at the front. It was just as if someone had crept in, not wanting to be heard. So I peeked round the door, and the sight I saw made my blood run cold. (*She points an accusing finger at Lizzie*) Her! That's who I saw. Standing over the body of poor Mrs Borden, she was, with an axe held in both hands, laughing like a crazy woman as she struck, and struck, and struck . . . (*She simulates emotion as best she can*) I hid at the bottom of the stairs and saw her leave the room, putting on her shoes, and lifting up her skirt, so she wouldn't leave a trail of blood. (*Defiantly, to Lizzie*) And that's why I was out in the yard being sick for so long!

Emma (*calmly*) Why didn't you tell all this to the police?

Bridget Ah, there I did wrong, to be sure. But I was weak, and when she offered me the money to see me loved ones in the old country, if I kept quiet, I didn't stop to think of the wrong I'd be doing. (*To Lizzie*) There! I know I promised never to speak a word of what I saw, but you've asked for it, with your filthy insults and accusations this evenin'.

Lizzie (*amused*) I'm quite sure Nance would have enjoyed that performance. But you haven't told Emma how I disposed of the axe, and clothing.

Bridget Surely you're not pretending you've forgotten?

Lizzie You know how it is—we old women, living on our own . . . ?

Bridget (*to Emma*) She was right, also, about me taking a bundle from the house. I did it for her. I took away the hatchet and dress.

Lizzie But, you said a short while ago I burned the dress . . .

Bridget Ah, I was merely sayin' what you'd paid me for. But I think my debt's been repaid now, and I'm free to speak me mind. (*Ominously*) And I'm thinkin' there'll be some as would like to know the truth.

Lizzie If you feel folk are interested in your version of the truth, don't hesitate on my account, Bridget. Maybe we could even arrange a fresh trial?

Bridget You wouldn't be after wanting that. This time they'd hang you.

Lizzie (*calmly*) Or you.

Bridget (*angrily, to cover her fear*) That's slanderous talk you're after makin', and I'm warnin' you I'm nobody's skivvy any longer, so watch your tongue!

Lizzie It's precisely because you were a "skivvy" that you're alive and able to stand there today talking to me. It was because you seemed a stupid, round-faced Irish maid that you escaped suspicion. Consider yourself one of the luckiest women in the world on that account, because your alibi didn't bear looking into!

Bridget I'll see a lawyer, that's what I'll do. It's malicious slander. First thing tomorrow I'll be there at his office. We'll see whose story they'll be believin'!

Lizzie It sounds like you've a busy day ahead of you.

Bridget You'll not be so clever then.

Lizzie Be careful not to over-estimate your own cleverness. (*Pointedly*) And now, as it's getting late, I think you ought to go and get some sleep. Then you'll feel fresh and clear-headed for your talk with the lawyer in the morning.

Bridget Oh, so it's throwing me out, ye are?

Lizzie (*after a pause*) It might be put that way, if you've a mind to it.

Bridget pauses, searching for a final taunt, but can think of none

Bridget Then good night to youse. (*She moves toward the french windows*)

Lizzie Not that way. You might get arrested as a common criminal.

Lizzie leads the way to the front door, with Bridget following. Bridget turns at the door for a last fling

Lizzie goes

Bridget (*to Emma*) You'd be wise to keep anything sharp locked up, and out of her way.

Bridget goes. A moment later the door is heard to shut, and Lizzie returns

Emma You think she'll go to a lawyer?

Lizzie (*shaking her head*) How else could she react?

Emma I couldn't bear another trial.

Lizzie We've both suffered enough for one life-time. (*She rings for the maid*)

Emma All the terrible things that would be said all over again.

Lizzie You've nothing to fear, Emma.

Emma Not that you seem to care much what folk say.

Lizzie I don't weep, if that's what you mean.

Emma Oh, I'm not blaming you, Lizzie . . .

Lizzie In which case, your sentiments are sharply at variance with your tone of voice.

Emma I've gone through all these years with mud clinging to me . . .

Lizzie You've said that once already this evening.

Emma I don't want more.

Lizzie I've assured you, Emma, that we'll never again hear from Bridget Sullivan, nor her lawyer. Now, please! I'm tired, and so are you. Let us not quarrel. (*She tugs again at the bell-rope*) What on earth's happened to Maggie?

Emma You're right, Lizzie. I am tired. I think I'll go to bed.

Maggie enters

Lizzie Where have you been?

Maggie (*sullenly*) Dressing. I was on my way to bed.

Lizzie Fetch a brush and pan. You can go to bed afterwards.

Sulkily, Maggie goes

Emma (*collecting up her embroidery*) I know I'm irritating at times . . .
Lizzie (*smiling*) Who isn't?
Emma I try not to be. It's just that—I still find you a little shocking. After all these years! Good night.

Lizzie kisses her

Lizzie Good night, Emma. God bless.
Emma Don't stay up too late.

Emma goes

Lizzie picks up the scrapbook and sits flicking through its pages

Maggie enters with a brush and pan

Lizzie There's some glass by the french windows that needs cleaning up.

Maggie goes to the windows and sweeps up the glass, slowly, as is her customary speed

Maggie Have you two been fighting again?

Lizzie considers answering, but changes her mind

She really will leave you one of these days! It's not just a threat. She'll go, and . . .
Lizzie That's enough, Maggie!
Maggie My name's not . . .
Lizzie (*still flicking through the book*) And on future occasions when we have visitors I'll thank you to remember your place and cut out such outrageous behaviour with the men.
Maggie (*poker-faced*) I don't know what you mean.
Lizzie You know perfectly well what I mean, so stop lying.

Maggie has finished her task, and stands up

Maggie You've no right to call me a liar!
Lizzie If you've finished cleaning up, go to bed.
Maggie You think you . . .
Lizzie I said that's enough! Go to bed!

Maggie moves toward Lizzie, her eyes blazing, the hand holding the brush raised, as if to strike a blow. Lizzie has her back to the maid, but senses the action. She remains perfectly still

Maggie pauses for a moment, then slowly walks from the room

Good night, Maggie.

The door is slammed. Lizzie stares thoughtfully at it, as—

the CURTAIN *slowly falls*

FURNITURE AND PROPERTY LIST

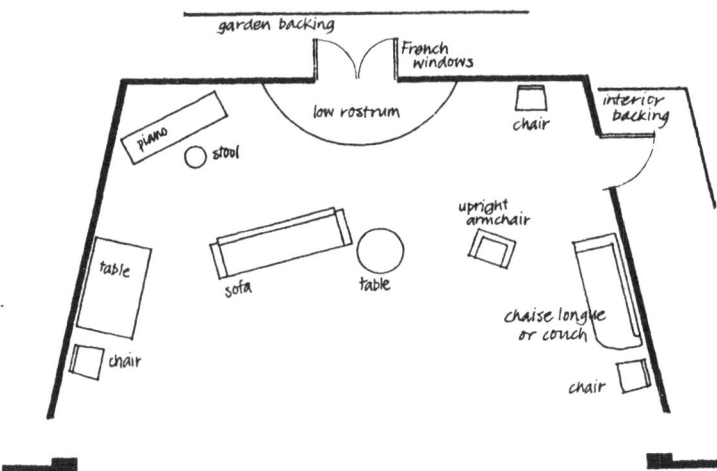

ACT I

On stage: Large table. *On it:* cloth, plates of sandwiches and other food, bowl
of punch and ladle, 8 glasses, lamp, napkins, cutlery
Small table. *On it:* **Emma's** embroidery
Sofa
Upright armchair
3 small chairs
Chaise-longue or couch
Upright piano. *On top:* lamp
Piano stool
On walls: mirror, bell-rope
Window curtains, almost closed
Carpet
Fender with fire-irons, including shovel

Off stage: Front door knocker (for use by **Cast**)
Large scrap album, duster (**Lizzie**)

ACT II

Set: Several used coffee cups, saucers, spoons, coffee-pot, on tray on food
table

LIGHTING PLOT

Property fittings required: 2 lamps, central light
Interior. A living-room. The same scene throughout

ACT I. Evening

To open: All interior lights on. Red glow from fire down c

Cue 1	Lizzie: ". . . not for the Borden family."	(Page 10)
	Fade to spot on **Lizzie**	
Cue 2	Lizzie: ". . . and went back into the house . . ."	(Page 10)
	Cross-fade to spot on **Annie**	
Cue 3	Lizzie: "He just laughed."	(Page 12)
	Cross-fade from **Nance** *to* **Annie**	
Cue 4	Nance: "What are you waiting for?"	(Page 12)
	Cross-fade to main Lights	
Cue 5	Lizzie: "And Emma's."	(Page 12)
	Fade to spot on **Annie**	
Cue 6	Sound of breaking glass	(Page 13)
	Cross-fade to main Lights	
Cue 7	Lizzie: ". . . at the doctor's entrance . . ."	(Page 16)
	Fade to spot on **Nance**'s *chair*	
Cue 8	Lizzie: ". . . was a mortician . . ."	(Page 19)
	Bring up spot on **Henry**	
Cue 9	Henry: ". . . life or death to him, Mr Borden!"	(Page 19)
	Fade spot on **Henry**	
Cue 10	Nance: ". . . not a very flattering thought, is it?"	(Page 20)
	Fade spot on **Nance** *slowly*	
Cue 11	Emma: ". . . the drug-store clerk, Eli Bence . . ."	(Page 20)
	Bring up spot on **Henry**	
Cue 12	Henry: "I'll be there."	(Page 21)
	Cross-fade to spot on a different area	
Cue 13	Tom: "That was Lizzie Borden."	(Page 22)
	Fade spot	
Cue 14	Emma: "Mean and cruel, every one!"	(Page 22)
	Bring up spot on **Annie** *and group*	
Cue 15	Emma: "That's a lie!"	(Page 23)
	Cross-fade to main Lights	
Cue 16	Emma: "William H. Medley offered evidence . . ."	(Page 24)
	Fade to spot on **Tom** *and* **Henry**	
Cue 17	Tom: "You bet I am."	(Page 24)
	Cross-fade to main Lights	

Cue 18	**Lizzie:** ". . . the problem of the blood . . ."	(Page 25)
	Fade to spot on **Nance** *and* **Henry**	
Cue 19	**Henry:** "How can the police be so blind?"	(Page 25)
	Cross-fade to main Lights	
Cue 20	**Lizzie:** ". . . around the search for bloodstains . . ."	(Page 27)
	Fade to spot on **Nance** *and* **Annie**	
Cue 21	**Emma:** "It's no good, Lizzie."	(Page 28)
	Cross-fade to main Lights	

ACT II.   Evening

To open:	As close of previous Act	
Cue 22	**Nance:** ". . . what went on after the arrest."	(Page 32)
	Fade to spot on **Annie**	
Cue 23	**Annie:** ". . . glared at one another."	(Page 33)
	Cross-fade to main Lights	
Cue 24	**Lizzie:** "Yes—the trial . . ."	(Page 33)
	Fade to spot on area for **Henry**	
Cue 25	**Henry** and **Tom** move out of spot	(Page 41)
	Cross-fade to main Lights	
Cue 26	**Lizzie:** ". . . like I said."	(Page 41)
	Fade to spot on area for **Henry**	
Cue 27	**Henry:** ". . . I am telling you."	(Page 42)
	Cross-fade to main Lights	

EFFECTS PLOT

ACT I

ACT II

Lightning Source UK Ltd.
Milton Keynes UK
UKOW06f0758100815

256677UK00003B/9/P